SPAN
OF
CONTROL

PRAISE FOR
SPAN OF CONTROL

"*Span of Control* is one of the best military themed leadership books I have ever read. Carey Lohrenz does a remarkable job of connecting success in the cockpit of a fighter jet with success in life. If you're going to buy one leadership book this year, make it this one!"

—ADMIRAL WILLIAM H. MCRAVEN
USN (retired)

"Filled with leading edge scientific research, captivating stories, and straightforward practices, Carey's direct, persuasive, and compelling call for each of us to focus on our span of control in the midst of uncertainty and tumultuous times makes this simply the right book, at the right time."

—STEVE FORBES
Editor-in-Chief and chairman of Forbes Media

"Carey Lohrenz has faced some of the most extreme environments imaginable in the cockpit at Mach 2. She also knows what challenge, high performance, and overcoming adversity—to not only survive, but thrive—looks like. An important book, *Span of*

Control gives you the valuable resources and concrete strategies as both a leader and a teammate to chart a better path forward and cultivate intense focus on what matters most."

—ALAN MULALLY

Former CEO of Boeing Commercial Airplanes;
Ford Motor Company

"As a Navy fighter pilot, Carey Lohrenz is an expert on conquering turbulence and prevailing in combat. In this book, she takes you inside the cockpit with vivid stories about how she excelled under pressure and practical lessons about how you can too."

—ADAM GRANT

#1 New York Times *best-selling author of* THINK AGAIN *and host of the TED podcast WorkLife*

"What I love and admire most about Carey Lohrenz is that she sees the possibility and potential in all of us to be positive difference-makers. In *Span of Control*, she shares a brilliant and brave model to help you navigate life's roughest waters and create meaningful change in order to thrive."

—KEN BLANCHARD

Coauthor of The New One Minute Manager*;* Servant Leadership in Action

"As Carey accurately points out, multi-tasking is a myth and will get you killed in combat. Snipers and pilots know it's all about focus and execution. Powerfully written, *Span of Control* is a must-read, and a major contribution to leadership."

—BRANDON WEBB
Former Navy SEAL
Entrepreneur
Multiple New York Times *best-selling author*

"Across areas and eras there are people who bend the arc of history because, quite simply, they *did what they could*. Cast into a crucible, they did not wilt, but rose to lead in ways that mattered most. *Span of Control* teaches you to lead by *doing what you can*."

—JAMES FELL
Author of On This Day in History Sh!t Went Down

"If I had one call to make in an emergency, Carey Lohrenz would be it. This is the right book for right now. At a time when distractions are endless and uncertainty surrounds us, *Span of Control* weaves together cutting-edge research and storytelling that reveals a better way to lead yourself, your family, your community, and your organization successfully. If you lead people, work with people—or, well, know any people—you must read this book!"

—MEL ROBBINS
Author of The 5 Second Rule *and four #1 audiobooks on Audible*
Daytime talk show host and tech entrepreneur
Presenter of one of the most viewed TEDx videos in the world

"I typically do not think of professional books as page-turners, but this one is. The book grabs you immediately—you feel like you are Carey's wingman as she lands her military jet on a bouncing carrier. You are not going to be able to put *Span of Control* down, but you should pace yourself and read it in timed increments to allow yourself the mental space to absorb important work and life lessons. Whether you are sixteen or one hundred years old, there is something for everyone in Carey's new book. *Span of Control* is a riveting, inspiring, and thought-provoking challenge to conventional thinking about success and high-performance—this is the perfect book for this turbulent time. Whether you're an aspiring young adult wanting to lead, or you're a professional leading a Fortune 100 company or a startup; if you're leading a sales team or your family or a volunteer group; this book will challenge you to rethink what is possible. In her well-researched, captivating, and witty book, Carey Lohrenz shows us the virtue of being able to adapt and overcome, and of learning both how to focus and navigate uncertainty and complexity."

—THERESA PAYTON
First female White House CIO
CEO of Fortalice Solutions
Author of Manipulated, *the #1 Hot New Release on Amazon and #1 2020 Nonfiction Best Seller at Independent Park Road Books*

Also by Carey D. Lohrenz

Fearless Leadership:
High-Performance Lessons From The Flight Deck

SPAN OF CONTROL

WHAT TO DO WHEN YOU'RE UNDER PRESSURE, OVERWHELMED, AND READY TO GET WHAT YOU REALLY WANT

CAREY D. LOHRENZ

ForbesBooks

Copyright © 2021 by Carey Lohrenz Enterprises, LLC.

Published by ForbesBooks, Charleston, South Carolina.
Member of Advantage Media Group.

ForbesBooks is a registered trademark, and the ForbesBooks colophon is a trademark of Forbes Media, LLC.

Printed in the United States of America.

10 9 8 7 6 5 4 3 2 1

ISBN: 978-1-95086-366-2
LCCN: 2021901740
Library of Congress Cataloging-in-Publication
data is available online or upon request.

Book design by Carly Blake.

This custom publication is intended to provide accurate information and the opinions of the author in regard to the subject matter covered. It is sold with the understanding that the publisher, Advantage|ForbesBooks, is not engaged in rendering legal, financial, or professional services of any kind. If legal advice or other expert assistance is required, the reader is advised to seek the services of a competent professional.

Since 1917, Forbes has remained steadfast in its mission to serve as the defining voice of entrepreneurial capitalism. ForbesBooks, launched in 2016 through a partnership with Advantage Media Group, furthers that aim by helping business and thought leaders bring their stories, passion, and knowledge to the forefront in custom books. Opinions expressed by ForbesBooks authors are their own. To be considered for publication, please visit **www.forbesbooks.com**.

For ordering information or special discounts for bulk purchases, please contact:
bookcarey@careylohrenz.com

To my kids, Danielle, Dalton, Annabelle, and Alexandra:
I'm deeply thankful to be a part of your journey. I have an
unshakeable confidence in your ability to be the light in any
storm and in your capacity to endure, and I know that you will
always be humble and gracious enough to put the ladder down
for those who might follow in your footsteps …

Love, Mom

CONTENTS

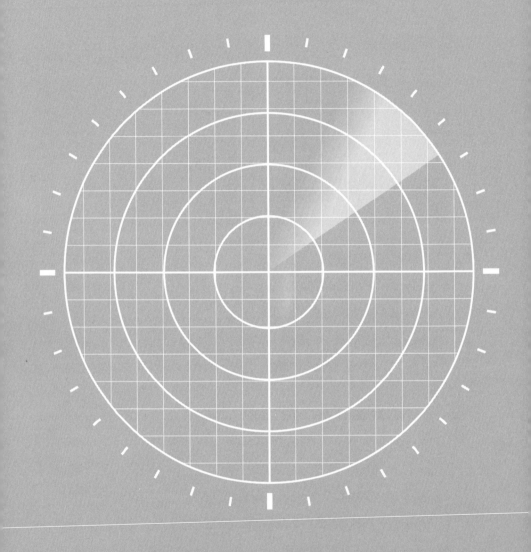

WHAT IS SPAN OF CONTROL?

My belief in the power of Span of Control as a mantra and a framework to help you adapt and flourish in demanding, grueling, and even heartbreaking situations was tested severely for me over the last couple of years.

2018 was a brutal year for me. A crucible of sorts.

In the middle of an unrelenting work travel schedule, I got the call: my mom was sick. She was diagnosed with pneumonia. After a week or two of not feeling much better, she went back to the doctor and was promptly hospitalized. As soon as I found this out, I flew straight from a speaking engagement down to Florida to be by her side. I assumed she would just be in the hospital for a couple of days. As each day passed, she grew weaker and weaker; inexplicably, her body began shutting down. It was clear something was not right. She had no appetite, was struggling to breathe, and the daily rigor of draining the fluid from her lungs was stealing any energy reserve she had.

For over two weeks straight, the doctors continued aggressively treating her with evermore powerful antibiotics, assuming she would "turn the corner." As they pumped her full of IV fluids *and* diuretics in an attempt to stabilize her condition, her legs—which were previously wisp-thin—and feet swelled to three times their normal size, and she could now no longer get out of bed and walk. This was demoralizing, because she needed to be able to walk on her own for them to release her from the hospital. During that time, I had work commitments that contractually I could not break, and I would fly back and forth from Orlando to my events, and right back to Orlando again—doing my best to compartmentalize and focus on what I could control *in the moment*. It was pneumonia after all. She should turn the corner soon, right? Thankfully, the doctors were letting my brother (who had flown in from out of town), her sister, and a sister-in-law visit and keep her company—but no one else, because they didn't want anyone else to "catch pneumonia" …

At about the twenty-fifth-day mark, the situation changed. After countless x-rays, blood draws, lung drains, cultures, and microscope readings, *by chance* an oncologist happened to take a peek at one of her culture slides. The answer was devastating.

Stage IV lung cancer.

Not pneumonia. Lung cancer.

We were devastated. And we needed answers. What kind of lung cancer was it? Had it spread? What treatment should there be? What are the next steps? Can we do chemotherapy? Can we do radiation? Can we get a second opinion? Where's the closest cancer center? What's the prognosis?

It felt like the world had stopped turning. And then it got worse. Because of a strange twist in Florida insurance law, my mom couldn't be transferred from the hospital directly to a cancer center. First, she had to be discharged … and in order to be discharged, she had to be able to walk. She couldn't, of course, due to the extreme swelling in her legs and weakened state overall.

So the doctors made the decision to discharge her to a physical therapy rehab center in hopes of her being able to regain some strength—enough to then be admitted to a cancer center.

During that time, I went home to see my kids for what I thought was going to be three to four days. I'd been either on the road or at the hospital for over a month, and had only seen them briefly at home one time. I flew home on a Wednesday night.

All day Thursday I spent working the phones, trying to find out why she couldn't get a PET scan while she was at the rehab center. After countless calls, finally a nurse discovered the problem. Somehow, there was a mistake on my mother's paperwork that said, "do not schedule PET scan until after discharge," when in fact it should've been done while she was at the hospital. By Thursday night, twenty-four hours after arriving at the physical rehab facility, no specialists had checked in on her, and she'd had no fluids or food.

Starting early Friday morning, armed with a stiff cup of coffee, hair piled on top of my head, I hit the phones again. I was focused on what mattered, and I was on a mission. I was desperately trying to find a workaround and to get a plan in place: to get my mom fully diagnosed and at least comfortable until we could figure out an answer to the question, "What next?"

I made an appointment at a local imaging center to have a "self-pay" PET scan done on my mom. I set up transportation to and from her physical rehab center. I called cancer centers in Tampa trying to figure out the admissions processes. I called patient advocates and other oncologists as well.

While I was on the phone with another doctor asking for him to advocate for an immediate transfer, again, I got the call: my mom had collapsed. They were taking her back to the hospital.

I hung up, booked a flight back down to Orlando, threw clean workout gear into my not-yet-unpacked suitcase, showered, and was out the door in less than forty-five minutes. Boarding that flight took every ounce of courage, grace, and composure I could muster. With my background in aviation, protocols, and security, I knew that if I looked even a *little* out of sorts, the flight crew could deny boarding, and I might not make it to the hospital in time to see my mom.

The realization that I had *been here before* was almost too much to bear. Just ten years prior, I found myself on a flight home to see my dad, who, after a surgery had gone awry, was clinging to life and on life support until I could make it to see him. It took three legs and several airport delays to get there. Just minutes after I walked through the door to his hospital room, he was gone.

And here I was, again … *again* … wondering if I would make it in time to see my mom alive or if I would be too late. The tears would not stop. I kept telling myself, "Span of Control, Span of Control, Span of Control … " I was blanketed in grief, and as I sat silently sobbing, a flight attendant simply touched my shoulder, handing me a three-inch stack of single-ply napkins. By the time we reached ten-thousand feet, my tears had melted through every napkin he had given me. That said, Span of Control was the buoy that kept me afloat—barely—but afloat, nonetheless. In that moment, it helped me to focus on the present, navigate what "could be," and simply sit in the vulnerability of not knowing what may lie ahead. What I know to be true is that calm is contagious, and panic-stricken, or grief-stricken, people do not make good decisions. I had to keep my nose above the waterline.

While airborne, I learned my mom had been intubated in the ambulance on the way to the hospital. I now had to wrap my head around the fact that I may not ever hear her voice again.

The next three days were a blur. Hoping. Watching blood pressure numbers. Praying. Counting breaths per minute. Planning. Waiting for blood gas readouts.

While in the intensive care unit, and while my mom was still intubated, a big, burly trauma doctor (who also happened to be an oncologist), pulled me aside. Apparently one of the nurses had passed along to him my questions about getting a PET scan. "Why do you think she needs a PET scan?" he asked.

I answered, "Because we need to know how bad this is. We still don't know. And we need to have a plan. Should she come home and sit outside in the sunshine, and just be comfortable? Do I bring her home with me? What kind of treatment should she have? Can she do chemo? What are we looking at? We need a plan."

He grew quiet, and then there was a long pause. "It's everywhere," he said. "She's not leaving here. I don't know if she'll even make it another five days."

I thought I was going to evaporate.

I remember saying under quiet gulps of air, "Then I guess we need a new plan. Thank you." I turned and walked back into my mom's room, held her hand, and listened to the rhythm of the ventilator doing the work for her. I had to focus on just being with her during what little time was left.

Over the next two days, the team worked nonstop trying to manage her vitals, her breathing, and her oxygen levels. The goal, the plan, was to see if they could get her to the point that they could extubate her, so she could at least speak again. They were able to wean my mom off the sedation meds just enough to be lucid. At this point, her tiny, frail hands, swollen from IVs and having her wrists wrapped (as is customary for those on ventilators, so they don't try to yank it out), motioned she wanted to communicate. As she made a pen-writing motion, the nurse brought in a Ouija-board-looking alphabet chart. For patients coming out of sedation, writing is too hard, so they use point-to-spell letter boards instead.

As tears welled up in her eyes, my mom slowly "typed" out the words, "I AM DONE."

A few hours passed, when she could finally manage a whisper. The last words my mom said to me were, "I love you. I'll see you soon, but not too soon."

She was gone not even twenty-four hours later.

The next few months would end up being punctuated by loss. After losing my treasured mom, I also lost a beloved uncle and an adored aunt. I had a relentless travel schedule, followed by massive job upheaval, and a health crisis of my own. All that was the perfect combination of things that could potentially blow me off course.

And I would have been blown off course, *if* I didn't know how to recognize overwhelm, acknowledge my vulnerabilities, focus on what matters most, formulate a flight plan to make the best possible decisions I could, and then communicate my intentions clearly. Then, deep breath, and carry on. Some days were daunting. The challenges were real, depleting every reservoir I had built up, both emotionally and physically.

Why I Wrote This Book

We all experience crucibles in our lives. They are traumatic, life-changing events that can end up shaping not only the way you lead, but the person you will become. Sometimes, the obstacles can seem insurmountable. Even worse, they can leave you bitter, hardened, resentful—stuck—if you don't know a way forward.

If you haven't experienced your life's crucible yet, I'd encourage you to take the time now to learn from those who have. My hope is that *Span of Control* will be the foundation, the operating manual of ideas, insights, and actions for your flight plan for success, come whatever may.

Globally, we are experiencing a profoundly tumultuous time. From pandemics to politics, the pace of change is accelerating so rapidly, our three- or five-year plans and prognostications seem almost, well, *laughable*.

And yet we are still here, we are still hopeful, and we know deep down that there must be a smarter way forward. None of us wants to just scrape by, muddle in mediocrity, or weather the storm only to end up *right. back. where. we. started.*

NONE OF US WANTS TO JUST SCRAPE BY, MUDDLE IN MEDIOCRITY, OR WEATHER THE STORM ONLY TO END UP *RIGHT. BACK. WHERE. WE. STARTED.*

At our cores, we may know we've lost some control. Some of us may even be facing deep uncertainty, having loosened our grip on what we *really* want and who we *really* want to be—as leaders, as teammates, as friends and family members.

For over thirty years, I've lived, studied, and researched leadership, high-performance behaviors, risk management, and human factors in all kinds of organizations. There is no doubt in my mind: these are challenging times.

I'm writing this book as someone who's been in one of the most demanding and high-pressure environments on earth—the cockpit of an F-14. That's where I learned some of my most unforgettable lessons not just in flying, but also in life and in leadership. My journey to that cockpit gave me indispensable insights as well. And my path after leaving the military—working among business leaders from Fortune 500 and *Forbes* Global 2000 executives to middle managers, from business owners to entrepreneurs to high-performing athletes—has helped me further distill those lessons in life and leadership, share them with others, and then watch as leaders and their teams flourish.

In my first book, *Fearless Leadership,* I described many of the lessons learned during my journey from growing up in a small town in the Midwest to getting into the cockpit of a $45 million fighter jet. I was struck then, and continue to be now, by the parallels between the world of naval aviation and the world of business. In both, leaders must perform highly complex and high-pressure tasks in a constantly changing environment. People are counting on you to make the right moves. Mistakes can result in huge financial losses or damage to your career. But no parallel has asserted itself more strongly or more consistently than this one: *high-performing teams require fearless leaders.*

No matter your situation, the number-one way to ensure that you're the best leader you can be is to build your ability to work through fear and do what needs to be done *in spite of* that fear. The ability to work through fear kept me alive as I operated under dangerous conditions and in life-or-death situations on the flight deck of that aircraft carrier, and it's what keeps any leader relevant, respected, and moving forward. If you're able to shape the fear into something useful, you'll be unstoppable.

Today we are living in an age of overwhelming chaos, and it's taking a toll on all of us: leaders, owners, educators, entrepreneurs, parents, partners, students. Every day there's more to do and less time to do it. We all make to-do lists in the morning and are lucky if we have three items crossed off by 5:00 p.m. We struggle to keep up with overflowing inboxes or persistent things to do. We're getting pulled in a million directions by work and social and family obligations, and it's all set to the chimes of our phones and the drone of upsetting news reports of events taking place, some thousands of miles from where we sit, some just down the street.

That's why, in this book, I want to build on insights from *Fearless Leadership*—the timeless traits of good leaders, ways of building resilience, and other best practices—and apply them to situations like the one most of us find ourselves in now, situations that demand that we identify what is still within our control during a time of chaos and upheaval, and the breakdown of systems on which we have come to rely. The biggest challenge, and opportunity, of the moment is learning how we can overcome our circumstances instead of being overwhelmed by them.

THE BIGGEST CHALLENGE, AND OPPORTUNITY, OF THE MOMENT IS LEARNING HOW WE CAN OVERCOME OUR CIRCUMSTANCES INSTEAD OF BEING OVERWHELMED BY THEM.

These are interesting times, no doubt, and our responsibilities can seem to grow heavier and heavier as a result. Do not become dispirited.

My message to you here is this: there are real opportunities for success even during times of crisis and uncertainty. As you read through the captivating stories, straightforward exercises, and research shared here, you'll find tools and tactics that you can bring to your home life, your workplace, your teams and other organizations— really any group that you're a part of. I've always argued that leadership is not just a matter of given titles or positions of influence. We are all leaders in some sense, which means that regardless of rank, succeeding when the pressure is on comes down to knowing what we can—and what we cannot—control.

In order to solve the problems raised by chaos, change, and uncertainty, in order to make our commitments, goals, and dreams happen, we've all got to recognize and be able to take advantage of opportunities to lead—to gather ourselves and our teams around clearly stated and achievable goals.

This means we need to learn to identify our priorities, find focus, and navigate obstacles. We need a flight plan for success that gives us a shot at harnessing all those skills, passions, and capabilities that we possess, a plan that brings them to the table so that we can tamp down the stress, find our joy, and not only survive, but *thrive*—as individuals and leaders striving for high performance in any area.

The foundational tenet of this book, Span of Control, is about knowing the number of things and the kinds of things you can—and should—effectively manage at any given time. As you'll see in the chapters that follow, your Span of Control is not set in stone. Span of Control changes as situations change and as abilities grow and transform.

I assure you this isn't pie-in-the-sky thinking. It's a high-octane dose of practicality and encouragement to get and to stay focused.

Through my own personal stories, as well as those of people from all walks of life who have overcome barriers of their own, I hope to give you the skills and tools necessary—as well as *the permission*—to write your flight plan for success and leverage your Span of Control, no matter your situation. I want you to have the framework and the knowledge to develop your confidence and the belief that no matter what happens, you'll figure it out, *and* you can go beyond whatever you thought was possible.

Together we're going to see how leaders of all kinds have used the principle of Span of Control, without even having a name to put to it, in order to overcome adversity and walk unexpected paths.

We're going to dive into eye-opening science and discover how your brain works in times of extreme stress, uncertainty, and chaos.

And we're going to work through proven practices, tools, and exercises that can help you cut through the noise, gain actionable insights, and leverage your Span of Control so that you can focus on the issues most relevant and meaningful to you.

In Part I, we'll address the fundamental signs of crisis and challenges to identifying our Span of Control. We'll look at how those challenges play out in real life, what we can do to recognize them, and how we can work to minimize them.

In Part II, we'll turn to matters of mindset and the ways that individually or collectively shifting our mindsets can powerfully affect our capacity to face down challenges and move our lives in the direction of our goals.

Part III is a call to action. We'll turn outward from that earlier work to focus on creating a personal action plan for success that can also be scaled to meet the needs of groups, teams, and organizations of all kinds. You'll learn

- how to set a clear vision and create a flight plan for success,

- how to communicate that vision and translate it into concrete goals and achievable "to do's," and

- how to break through to a whole new level of what's possible.

Most important, you'll learn how all this can be achieved *even in the midst of a period of intense challenges or serious crisis.* In order to solve the challenges of chaos and make our goals, dreams, and commitments a reality, we have to understand that to succeed when the pressure is on and improve our performance overall, we've got to know what we can and cannot control.

I'll tell you right here and remind you throughout this book: you have the capability to cope with, deal with, grapple with, contend with, master, maintain, sustain, retain, conserve, preserve, tackle, and overcome all that life has to throw at you.

For each of us, it all comes down to awareness of our Span of Control.

YOUR SPAN OF CONTROL FRAMEWORK

- Focus on what matters most. (Identify your top three things, and remove distractions.)

- Formulate a flight plan for success. (Prepare, perform, prevail: never leave success to chance.)

- Communicate what's possible. (Make it concise, precise, clear, and consistent.)

PART I
SIGNS OF CRISIS

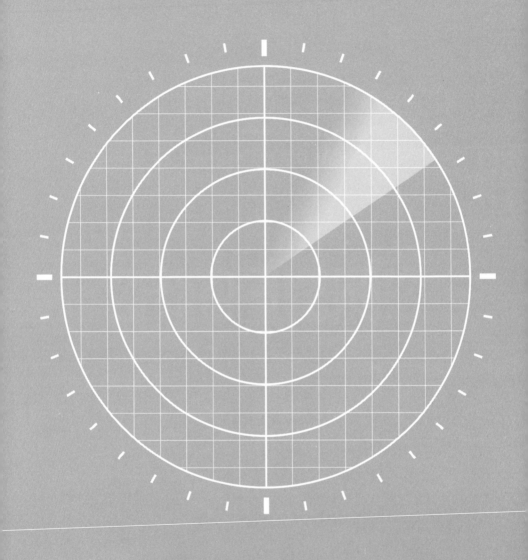

Chapter 1

TASK OVERLOAD

'm about to land my Tomcat, a supersonic twin-engine fighter jet, on the deck of an aircraft carrier. It's one of the most dangerous maneuvers in all of aviation. That alone would be enough—my runway is shifting on the crest of each wave, and it feels like I am trying to fit an elephant through a keyhole—but it's also the middle of the night, and the darkness is disorienting. As I fall from the sky at hundreds of feet per minute, I can barely see lights on the carrier, and there's no hint of a horizon.

All I see is inky blackness.

The line of glowing points on the deck tilts side to side in a slow seesaw motion. The countdown begins. At three quarters of a mile, the landing signals officer (LSO) pipes up: "One zero five, on and on, three quarters of a mile. Call the ball."

My radar intercept officer (RIO) answers, "One zero five, Tomcat ball, five-point-seven, Lohrenz."

I steel myself, trusting my relentless preparation, practice, and experience to stifle the burning fear in the pit of my stomach. I don't want to hit the water or the back end of the carrier—what we call a "ramp strike."

The LSO calmly replies, "Roger ball, Tomcat, wind is twenty knots."

Inside the cockpit, my RIO is calling out our rate of descent in feet per minute: "Six hundred … six fifty … six hundred … six hundred … six hundred … " The goal is to be steady, on speed, on glide path to assure a safe landing.

As adrenaline courses through my veins and sweat wets my brow, my attention is pulled in a thousand different directions. In this moment, there are so many things outside of my control—the gusty winds, the overpowering darkness, the crashing waves, the moving target. But thanks to that dedicated training and preparation, I know to focus on three—and only three—critical things: meatball, line up, and angle of attack.

MEATBALL, LINE UP, AND ANGLE OF ATTACK

1. **Meatball**: the orangey light that tells me how close I am to the optimal glide path (i.e., either high or low).

2. **Line Up**: you "line up" on the centerline of the landing area of a carrier—a particularly challenging task, because it is canted seven degrees to the port side compared to the ship's centerline. In order to stay on centerline, the pilot must continually correct to the right.

3. **Angle of Attack (AOA)**: my wings' angle in relation to the relative wind (on any aircraft, too great an AOA will cause the wing to stop flying, i.e., stall, as airflow across the top is disrupted). This angle determines how far the aircraft tailhook hangs below the eye of the pilot. Since every aircraft is different, it is critical for the

pilot of each aircraft to fly "on speed" so the hook doesn't move up or down and so that it catches the appropriate arresting wire as the aircraft touches down aboard the carrier.

It takes extreme hand-eye coordination, focus-shifting ability, and the resolve to *hang in there no matter what*, but I know that if I can take care of those three things—meatball, line up, angle of attack—I can increase my chances of landing safely. At this moment, those three things are what's within my Span of Control. Not the wind. Not the ocean. Not what my commander said that morning. Not what I'll do tomorrow. Just meatball, line up, angle of attack. They *intentionally* become my whole world as my focus shifts from one to the other at hyperspeed, hitting each of those things at nearly ten times a second!

Meatball. *Next.* Line up. *Next.* Angle of attack.

Boom! We hit the deck. I'm going 145 knots, nearly 170 miles per hour, when the arresting hook on my Tomcat snags a wire. I slam both throttles to full military power and click my speed brakes in, just in case my hook doesn't fully engage the arresting wire, or the wire snaps and I have to attempt to get flying again. My body is slammed forward with such force that it feels as if my arms and legs are going to separate from my body. I come to a full stop in 1.2 seconds.

We've landed.

These landings are like controlled car crashes. The touchdown is enough to destroy most other airplanes—but not the F-14. United States Navy and Marine Corps fighter pilots are the *only* fighter pilots in the world who will land high-speed fighters on and off aircraft carriers at night. No one else in the world will even make the attempt.

As you can imagine, there is a little bit of pressure.

Operating in the Pacific Ocean theater, you get the opportunity to experience some of the most treacherous swells and rollers found anywhere in the world. Oftentimes the backend of the aircraft carrier can be up and out of the water thirty-five to forty feet. Now, that may not seem like a big deal, but when you are coming aboard an aircraft carrier at nearly 170 miles per hour and you only have about six to eight feet of clearance to begin with? You have yourself an angles problem. The first time you see the back end of a carrier up and out of the water during the daytime, you'll find your humility or your Jesus, whatever that may be.

Now imagine that same scenario *at night,* when you are a thousand miles away from shore and you cannot control the environment. Not the weather. Not the ship. Not your tasking. Not your communication system. Not your aircraft systems. Not your teammates' reaction to stress.

Even for an experienced fighter pilot, night carrier landings are always a challenge. It never gets easy, nor should it. This isn't landing on a ten-thousand-foot runway—this is landing on a bobbing three-hundred-foot-long … postage stamp.

The risks are high. There will always be uncertainty and uncontrollables—even catastrophes—that we have to work through. *Risk is unavoidable when you are pushing the performance envelope*—that is true in both fighter aviation and in life.

The only thing you can do to ever so slightly mitigate the tension and anxiety? Do it again. Over and over and over.

The good news is that learning to focus on our Span of Control is a skill available to us all. That repetitive practice, the relentless preparation, is all about pinpointing what is in our hands in order to make the best decisions possible. That's why all fighter pilots, and many of the rest of us, resolve to be constantly learning. We continually leverage our experience, gather new insights and information, prepare and train for a better outcome.

Despite what some might want you to think, no one shows up on day one a fully qualified military fighter pilot—not even those folks who show up with hundreds of hours of civilian flight time thinking they are all that and a bag of chips.

Here's how the training works: starting on day one, whether at the Naval Academy, in your ROTC program, or at Aviation Officer Candidate School, the training is a set of building blocks, one skill learned after another and always under some sort of pressure—fatigue, physical stress, academic stress, sleep deprivation—you name it. And, like most anything else, first you have to learn how to crawl, then walk, then run. The ultimate goal is to be able to operate successfully in extreme conditions: air-to-air combat, high-speed intercepts, close air support for ground forces, photo reconnaissance, and eventually, landing on the aircraft carrier at night. Under pressure, you don't simply rise to the occasion—you sink to the level of your training.

UNDER PRESSURE, YOU DON'T SIMPLY RISE TO THE OCCASION— YOU SINK TO THE LEVEL OF YOUR TRAINING.

Or at least that's the idea.

But I'm getting way ahead of myself: first you have to make it through all of the phases of flight school that will even get you to that point. Flight training for a naval aviator takes around twelve to twenty-four months, depending on your training pipeline, i.e., aircraft designation (helicopters, propeller aircraft, or strike fighters [jets]). And in each phase—Primary, Intermediate, and Advanced—we had demanding academic classes and tests, were often flying multiple flights a day, and were constantly being evaluated.

As much as someone might've wanted to be a naval aviator, the funnel narrowed through attrition at each phase. While only the top

10 percent of each Primary class even had a shot at selecting the strike fighter pipeline—or getting into the strike fighter pipeline—even that didn't mean you would get a slot. Ultimately, that decision was based on a combination of your grades and the "needs of the Navy." So, competition was fierce from the get-go. It takes about two years, the longest of all training pipelines, to earn the coveted gold naval aviator wings in the strike fighter pipeline.

The good news?

Starting in Advanced Strike Fighter Training, we begin training to fly low and fast. Honestly, that was some of the most fun flying I've ever done. The speed rush is incredible; the adrenaline courses through your veins. You're darting in and out of mountains and rolling through valleys. It's a million-dollar ride each and every time.

Clearly, though, this type of flight in a low-altitude environment is both *high workload* and *high risk*. We've been training nonstop for almost two years in high-workload, high-stress environments, developing coping mechanisms, techniques, and tricks before we even get to this point. The Naval Air Training Command's *Flight Training Instruction for Low Altitude Awareness* says this kind of mission "is an environment in which *task saturation* can overtake a pilot before there is clear awareness of developing danger." Task saturation or task overload is what happens when the number of things an aviator is asked to pay attention to outpaces the information-processing capacity of the brain. In other words, when there are way too many things begging for the pilot's attention, if he or she were to focus on all of them, it would result in a major accident that would likely result in loss of life.

I share this with you so you can imagine what it is like to land on an aircraft carrier at night in the pitch-black inky darkness, or be whistling through the desert low and fast at speeds illegal in most every other part of the country, with less than a third of a second margin for error or time to impact. The lack of certainty. The anxiety. The tension. The adrenaline. The fear. The excitement. Everyone has a different physiological response to that fear. Some people taste it. Some people sweat. Some people vomit; some people vurp (a vomit burp). Other people's hearts race. Some get goose bumps.

You'd be hard pressed to find an aviator whose palms haven't gotten sweaty, who hasn't felt that numbing, aching, pit-in-the-stomach feeling, who hasn't gone around several times in the pattern after failing to trap (to land), specifically during nighttime carrier operations.

It's happened to me. I've felt it. We all have. We even have a saying for it. We call it having your "night in the barrel."

But all of us have to figure out how we are going to work through those feelings if we want to be successful. How do we maintain our focus on what's most important, when just a moment's

HOW DO WE DEVELOP OUR CAPACITY FOR TARGETED AWARENESS?

inattention could mean catastrophe? In particular, how do we develop our capacity for targeted awareness?

The goal is to avoid ever reaching the point of debilitating task saturation, to keep a clear view of current and developing dangers, and to be able to complete your mission objective.

We've all experienced the feelings of dread, overwhelm, frustration, and stress, feeling like we're drowning in too much to do with not enough time, tools, or resources to get the job done. Whether that overwhelm comes from information overload (too-much-data syndrome) or technical skill overload (when our brains prioritize and focus on a single thing in an attempt to regain control, to stabilize the situation), when you then throw in a handful of accelerating changes, stress, anxiety, and a pandemic? The net result is the same: the average person's ability to multitask, or task switch, goes right out the window.

That stress, that anxiety, narrows our perceptual field, limiting our ability and capacity to process any new information.

That stress can reduce the capacity of our working memory and inhibit information recall and long-term memory. In what's known as the "strong but wrong effect," stress can even cause you to revert to previously learned behaviors that may or may not be effective. Collectively, stress and anxiety conspire to thwart your ability to get the darn job done and can bring you dangerously close to being unable to execute your well-thought-out plan.

The military has spent a lot of time and money researching and mitigating task overload, and the most surprising thing, discovered early on, was that typically pilots weren't even aware of its onset. They would reach cognitive overload and hit the ground (literally crash!) before they even knew what was happening.

But fighter pilots have developed coping mechanisms, techniques, and tricks that allow us to work through extraordinarily high task loads while under extreme stress. Which brings us to today and my need to share with you information about how to focus in on your Span of Control.

You might already be familiar with use of the term in the corporate world, where your Span of Control is the number of direct reports you can effectively manage at one time. But in the Navy, the idea is a lot broader and a lot bigger—even though the phrase itself is not regularly used.

Your Span of Control is determined by the things you can, and should, control at any given time. Everything else is just a distraction.

Span of Control is how we reminded ourselves what to focus on right in the moment, knowing that anything else was outside our

Your Span of Control is determined by the things you can, and should, control at any given time. Everything else is just a distraction.

—CAREY LOHRENZ

control and shouldn't take up precious mental space. Recognizing our Span of Control kept us focused on what mattered most and became a primary tool in taming the distractions and pressures of flying demanding, high-pressure missions. In the Navy, your Span of Control not only kept you *alive*, it kept you loving your job and kept your mission and purpose clear.

But for me, Span of Control is more than a term—it's a mantra.

Over the years, this mantra took up residence in my soul and has been one of the biggest driving forces and motivators in my life—so much so I have "SOC" inked on the inside of my right wrist. Every time I feel overwhelmed, I glance down at those three letters to remind myself that I can only control so much and that the best way to conquer the chaos is to stay focused on those things I truly can control, right now, in this moment.

Why SOC? Why not just *focus* in pretty script? Why not *concentrate* or *meditate* in Sanskrit?

Because it's specific, it's intentional, and it's *actionable*.

As I covered in-depth in *Fearless Leadership,* **action conquers fear.**

Not just some glittery platitude, "Span of Control" has been the strategy, tool, framework, compass—*the guiding force*—that's kept me sane, focused, and on task. It's quelled depression, anxiety, and stress. It's guided me through loss, grief, and heartache. It's kept me excited about the things I am passionate about and eliminated the things that brought me down. It's allowed me to see what could be, while navigating what is.

IT'S ALLOWED ME TO SEE WHAT COULD BE, WHILE NAVIGATING WHAT IS.

And it saved my life more than one dark night above the choppy Pacific Ocean.

Overwhelmed and Overworked

While you may never find yourself in the cockpit of a Tomcat repeating a mantra that sounds more like an order at your local Italian restaurant than a lifesaving or business-saving technique, you've no doubt felt moments of being overwhelmed, overworked, stressed out, bummed out, and desperately needing something definitive to hold on to.

As a mom of four, wife, business owner and consultant, board member, and speaker to audiences across the globe, I'll be the first to say that the stress here on land can be nearly as intense as the stress forty thousand feet up in the air.

We live in an age of overwhelming chaos, and it's taking a toll on all of us. Pre-COVID-19, on the lecture circuit, I was speaking over a hundred times a year while also raising a family, running a business, and serving on boards. That's a lot to manage under normal circumstances. Now that workload has shifted to my home, where events are running virtually.

Then, and perhaps even more so now, we are pulled in a million directions by work and social and family obligations, all of it set to the chimes of our iPhones and the drone of upsetting news reports.

Then and now, the unrelenting stream of information and our own propensity for doomscrolling is sapping our energy. We are feeling devastated by life's never-ending disappointments, especially those that come at us out of left field. We feel frazzled or disengaged or bored or just plain scared.

I know I didn't sit at my kindergarten desk eating my Windmill cookies, drinking strawberry milk, dreaming of the day I'd sit in a traffic jam in an Uber, stressed almost to tears about being so late that I was about to miss the last flight home of the day after being on the road for weeks on end. On the playground way back when, we didn't hope to one day lose three hours on Facebook, jealously scrolling through an ex-friend's newsfeed and bitterly, silently cursing him or her over a recent promotion. None of us dreamed of listening to last week's presentation on our headphones and sending emails a week late all while cheering on little Tommy at the soccer game (and you just missed him make that goal again, didn't you?).

Certainly, most of us didn't expect a pandemic would literally shut down our businesses overnight with no warning, or that we'd be expected to virtually homeschool our kids while still working full time, or that we'd be running our businesses virtually, or even looking for a new job—any job.

It's just too much.

Years ago, our family had just moved to a new town out of state where we knew almost no one, and my husband was regularly gone for work for two weeks at a time. Meanwhile, I was wrangling four kids under seven years old and dealing with the oldest two being in new, different schools. We'd put our just-moved-into house back on the market after only a few months after realizing it literally sat in a snake nest (yikes); there were afterschool activities, nonstop house showings (house not selling, market diving—a perfect real estate shitstorm); I had volunteered for the PTA, Lord help me; and my dad had been critically injured in a snowmobiling accident 1,068 miles away.

And then two of my kids ended up having to have surgery. All. At. The. Same. Time.

Frankly, at the time, I thought I was "handling it."

I'm of Dutch and Hungarian immigrant grandparents. We don't complain. We don't fuss. We don't do drama. We simply work. We endure. We are Midwestern stoicism at its finest.

And I *was* handling it all—in a sense. No outbursts, no yelling. I was getting it all done. I was keeping my shit together. *chef's kiss*

Clean house. Check. Permission slips. Check. Parent volunteering. Check. Kids fed fruits and vegetables? Check, check. Work. Check. Workout. Meh, mostly. Check. Business and work still staying on track. Check. Survival mode.

But I wasn't "handling it." I was simply keeping it all in and grinding, trying to do it all—because that's what Type As do, right? I was trying to multitask at the macro level of my life.

Kids, health, parents, husband, friends, work.

I had to get the oldest kids back and forth to school on time, keep the house spotless for showings, attempt to get "regular naps" in for the babies (parents of kids under two, I can hear you laughing and raising your wineglass, water bottle, or high-five at me right now). I had to navigate a new city and new neighbors with an often-gone spouse, attend PTA meetings, worry about kids' specialist appointments and surgeries—all on top of the sadness and helpless feeling of having an injured and ailing parent a thousand miles away. With no support system. No family nearby, no babysitters yet in this strange town.

Eventually, it became too much. Even though I was what most would consider "stress-hardy," stress started to affect my health—slowly, insidiously. The nonstop nights of interrupted sleep or no sleep. The worrying about everyone else's health. A newborn. (I mean, just one three-hour straight sleep night would've felt like a gift.)

I longed for the simpler days at Aviation Officer Candidate School, those sixteen weeks of endless and enormous physical, psychological, and academic stress and training, testing every bit of my strength, commitment, and stamina. Those were weeks of sleep deprivation, trash cans slinging down the hallway, twelve-mile runs, trying to stay awake in class, waiting to hear the voice of my drill instructor bellow "Just begin!" and other DIs popping out from behind bushes, dumpsters, you name it. The creative ways they would trip you up, then grind you down—physically, mentally, emotionally. That all seemed … "simpler." Doable. I understood that it made you stronger if you could manage it. And if you were successful, there was a known end point: graduation.

There is no "end point" when you have four little kids, own a business, and have made everyone else a priority. I loved my life, my kids, my husband—*and* I was running on fumes. I started having erratic racing heart episodes. Then there were several episodes of indiscriminately feeling like I might pass out. Neither of which had ever happened before.

Ever.

I had been a D-1 athlete, a rower at the University of Wisconsin–Madison. So, in addition to other great life lessons learned as a varsity athlete, I *knew* what feeling like I was going to pass out felt like. I knew about suffering from pain so intense it scrambles your thinking and every bit of survival logic is telling you to quit. Rowing at that level, constantly pushing max physical effort—even your eyes are affected by the effort—your vision goes full-on tunnel. You are convinced you might die. You're sure there is no way in hell you'll ever make it to the finish line or to the end of that 6K on a Concept2 Erg, and yet you manage.

I was a former fighter pilot, for Pete's sake! I pulled six to eight Gs! *shakes fist at sky*

No one has time for a meltdown. And I felt like no one wanted to hear about how tired or stressed or lonely or isolated or exhausted I might be, especially when my friends and family were still deployed. *Those* are valid problems, right? And mine were first world problems.

There was work to do, and I. Could. Handle. This.

Until I couldn't.

Some responses to stress and pressure are better than others. I discovered that keeping it all in, not asking for help, maintaining a full workload, operating as if everything was "ops normal," and trying to do it all—was not working. I ended up having to wear a Holter monitor to keep track of my heart rhythm and rate 24/7 for thirty days. The doctors realized that my heart rate was spiking to 170 beats a minute every day at certain pressure points like naptime, house showings, kids out the door and into four cars seats at a time, and bedtime.

Bedtime! Wait, what? That should be one of the easiest, most blissful times of the day, right?

It was like I was running a marathon and not even getting the benefits! I loved being a mom. I wasn't stressed about *that*! None of this made sense.

Mine wasn't simply a time-management problem. No snappy color-coded spreadsheet was going to help me handle everything. No life guru was going to fix this symptom by telling me to "block out some 'me time'" (I hear you moms and working parents out there snort-laughing at the concept of "me time"). This was a deadly situation, and something needed to change, or I wasn't going to be around to raise those four kiddos.

THIS WAS A DEADLY SITUATION, AND SOMETHING NEEDED TO CHANGE.

It surprised me to think that I was the same person who could fly a sophisticated piece of military equipment in all kinds of intense, high-risk situations! I had *years of training* on how to overcome profound levels of stress and navigate task saturation and task overload.

What was happening to me is known as stress-induced cardiomyopathy. It's sometimes referred to as "broken heart syndrome," because it can be brought on by a stressful event, such as the death of a loved one. Or it can occur because of relentless stress and profound exhaustion.

At the same time that I was starting to experience this physical symptom of overwhelm, another dear friend—a Marine Corps aviator and former flight school buddy—was killed during a training flight flying the F/A-18 Hornet. Sadly, and ironically enough, the cause was probable loss of situational awareness due to ... task overload.

From early on in our training as naval aviators, we hear the phrase "speed is life." As fighter pilots, we are continuously training to think critically, stay focused, make decisions at the speed of sound, to manage risk, maintain safety awareness and combat readiness, to stay ahead of the jet, stay ahead of the power curve. And here I was ... very clearly behind the curve.

I had lost my way. I was trying to do alllll the things (which is ridiculous, because no one can do it all) instead of only the most important things.

For one, it felt like everything mattered. I mean, *clearly* my kids being read to, fed, changed, napped, and sent off to school mattered, and *clearly* work getting done, staying connected with family, and selling the house mattered.

I can handle this. I can figure this all out.

But whew. I was overloaded. I was on a hamster wheel in relentless pursuit of getting everything done. I was beyond exhausted, and feeling like I had to have all these things done "perfectly" (whatever that actually means) was causing the stress to pile up even more. (I swear to you, hand over heart, I'm actually pretty chill!)

Most everything that had allowed me to be successful in the past was something I was *still doing*, but what I hadn't done was say "no" to the things that mattered *less*.

I got sucked into an almost deadly trap of thinking I was effectively multitasking *and* that I could do it all, continuously, on little sleep. In fact, I was task switching among way too many things, and I was beyond my physical capacity.

I didn't focus on what mattered most; I didn't say "no" to those things that were less important "for right now." I didn't write down a plan for the day or my flight plan for success. I didn't use a simple checklist to keep track of all the necessities, and I certainly did not communicate, delegate, or ask for help. The point here isn't to get into a comparison contest of "Oh yeah, you think that was hard? Well, I had to … " My situation was the perfect storm—for me. And yours may be too for you.

EVERYONE STRUGGLES, AND THERE IS A PATH FORWARD.

Everyone struggles, and there is a path forward.

How did I get back on track? I had to turn awareness into action.

I REFOCUSED ON MY SPAN OF CONTROL

- Every day I identified the top three most important things I had to get done.

- I wrote down my flight plan for success. I once again started using a simple checklist for target goals and I started "task shedding," saying "no" to whatever didn't help me get the most important things done.

- I started communicating about things I had been silent about. I started asking for help—with laundry and with babysitters for my kids' doctor's visits, so I wasn't having to wrangle all four at specialist appointments. And on the rare day when two of my kids were still napping when it was time to go to some fluffy school activity, I let them sleep. Why? Because that's what was better for all of us. One hundred percent worth it.

I won't say everything was suddenly sunshine and sunflowers, because it was still a lot of work.

The point here isn't to get into a comparison contest of "Oh yeah, you think that was hard? Well, I had to … " It's to share with you that everyone struggles and that there is a path forward.

Why is this important? Because right now we are driving ourselves into the ground. Literally. According to the American Heart Association, cardiovascular disease and heart health incidents continue to be both men *and* women's greatest health threat—killing one out of four men, and one out of five women annually.[1] And that affects us all, oftentimes with devastating results.

How can you find your path forward? Here are some questions you may find helpful.

FOCUS QUESTIONS

- What are the top three most important things *you* should be focusing on right now?

- When you think of your average day, what are the things that are within your Span of Control? List them.

- Is there something you need to say "no" to in order to have time and energy for what's most important to you?

Chapter 2

MULTITASKING IS A MYTH

Most of us, especially the Type As, like to think we're *great* multitaskers. (Remember when everyone was putting that description in their résumés?)

In this Age of Distraction, multitasking seems like a useful superpower to have, but unfortunately, it isn't even real—it's a myth. Or, as Shalena Srna from the University of Michigan puts it, *a false impression.* "Multitasking is often a matter of perception," she says, "or can even be thought of as an illusion."[2] When we *think* we're multitasking, we're actually just switching back and forth between two or more tasks in rapid succession; we're actually *task switching.* And there's often little rhyme or reason to our task switching. We dog paddle through the day doing whatever thing *feels* most pressing or *seems* the least taxing at the moment, and we let worries and distraction invade our flow of action.

For instance, maybe you should be focusing on writing that article (within your Span of Control), but instead you're obsessively refreshing Gmail to see if the magazine editor liked your pitch (not in your Span of Control) and checking Instagram to see if the photo of your cappuccino got good engagement (not in your Span of Control) or looking down at your incoming texts while on a Zoom call …

IF YOU'RE NOT PRIORITIZING AND DETERMINING WHICH IS MOST IMPORTANT— YOU'RE GOING TO EXPERIENCE THE SIGNIFICANT COSTS OF TASK SWITCHING.

You might even be trying to task switch among two or three things that really do matter. But inevitably, if you're not focusing on the thing *that matters most right now*—in other words, if you're not prioritizing and determining which is most important—you're going to experience the significant costs of task switching. This isn't just about lost time or productivity; task switching can be downright dangerous—to your mental health, your physical safety, or to that of your teammate, passenger, or patient.

Toggling back and forth between tasks doesn't just eat up time during each switch, it slows down and can even derail your mental progress for up to a half hour after.[3] In other words, that thirty seconds to send a text while you're right in the middle of something important isn't just thirty seconds down the drain—*it's thirty minutes and thirty seconds.*

And while all these distractions hurt productivity, they also have negative emotional effects.

Gloria Mark of the University of California, Irvine, has done several studies when it comes to task switching, distractions, and disruptions, including a comprehensive study of email use, productivity, and stress. "Our research has shown that attention distraction can lead to higher stress, a bad mood, and lower productivity," Mark wrote in the *New York Times.*[4]

In another of Mark's studies, observers were sent to shadow employees at several tech and finance companies for three and a half days. Researchers logged each worker's activities and timed every task to the second. They found people switch activities an average of every three minutes and five seconds. And guess what? *This was back in 2004.*[5]

That finding comes as no surprise to me. I lived it. Heck, I was lucky to get the shower water to turn hot before someone would yell, "MOM!" The idea of five whole minutes of uninterrupted solitude to think about implementing a strategy, or changing a culture, or just staying on task? That sounded like a luxury. And I paid a price when I started bypassing the things that had allowed me to be successful in the past. It wasn't intentional. It happened slowly, insidiously.

In 2016, Mark repeated the same study to discover that the median length of time on task had been cut down to—wait for it— *forty seconds*! Think about your average nine-to-five job. That's 720 toggles a day! When you combine that with knowing that it takes half an hour to reorient your focus—well, it's no wonder we're all so frustrated. We are working against ourselves!

In fact, we're very literally working against ourselves when we engage in self-inflicted interruptions. Working on a task and switching tabs to check Facebook, for example, is a self-inflicted interruption, whereas a coworker walking over to discuss a project is not. Regardless of the source of the interruption, the result is the same: we are, essentially, playing tennis with our cognitive energies, volleying them back and forth. Only unlike a bouncy tennis ball, our brains take more time to switch directions.

The fallout of rapid task switching goes beyond wasting time; it sacrifices some of our best thinking. **By switching our focus so often, we aren't allowing for deep thinking, for careful reflection, or for creative problem solving. Task switching also causes drops in IQ,** about the same as if you missed a night's sleep.[6]

Essentially, task switching is making us forgetful, dumber, and more stressed out.

That may explain why we feel like we're busier than ever but also getting nothing done. When we task switch, we dilute our focus. And when we dilute our focus, we dilute our power. (And ladies, don't buy into the related myth that women are better task switchers than men! That's a popular idea, but it's been soundly debunked.[7])

WHEN WE DILUTE OUR FOCUS, WE DILUTE OUR POWER.

WHEN WE TASK SWITCH:

- **We revert to bad habits.** We've all been guilty of half-following what's going on in a meeting while we work on our laptop or phone. "Bill's going to spend an hour on this PowerPoint," we think. "I might as well burn through some email." This might seem like a reasonable decision, but in making it, you have chosen to *fracture your focus* and follow the path of least resistance. When you do that, you have a host of bad habits and routines waiting to tempt you. "Why not check the stock market or Instagram?" you might think after shooting off a few replies.

- **We become less resilient.** If you're trying to write a draft of an article for a major trade magazine in your industry while having a half-hour Slack conversation with your boss about something else, you're going to drain your resources really fast. When you get stuck on the article (and you will get stuck), you'll be much more likely to throw your hands up in frustration and put it off to tomorrow … or never.

- **We miss out on important moments.** Task switching also keeps us from engaging in life. You know those parents on the sidelines of their kid's soccer, football, or lacrosse game, looking for the credit for showing up while spending 95 percent of their time heads down on their phones? Do you think they'll look back in twenty years and remember all the emails they caught up on?

- **We make mistakes.** Trying to do more than one thing at once is a good way to make sure you half-ass them both. Some of the mistakes we make are small and cause only minimal damage, like a typo in an email. But others have major consequences.

- **We weaken our ability to remember.** Heavy task switching— basically what we do when we're working on a spreadsheet, listening to a podcast, and checking Twitter or a news site every few minutes—is linked to underperforming on tasks of working memory and sustained attention.[8] How many of you struggle through a three-minute read online, only to notice afterward that you can't really account for what you just read?

When you start to experience that overwhelm, try using this tool:

HACK THE CLOCK

Often when we are panicked, we get time compressed—time seems to speed by out of control—which can lead to us making bad decisions.

"Hack the clock" is a term we use in aviation when a crisis or emergency pops up in-flight. We physically push a timer on our cockpit clock so that we have a realistic gauge on how much time is *actually* passing.

We intentionally slow things down to maintain a stable, safe, and operational environment.

Hacking the clock does two things for the aviator: (1) it provides us with an automatic physical reaction to crisis that reasserts our sense of control even as adrenaline is coursing through our veins, and (2) it triggers our memorized checklists or action steps.

It gives us time to assess the situation.

Hacking the clock helps us control that "fight, flight, or freeze" response. It allows our brains to catch up to the situation at hand.

Hacking the clock isn't just for fighter pilots. When you hit a sudden storm, hacking the clock is a tried-and-true method for slowing down, taking stock, and not letting this new level of chaos throw you off. During a crisis, noting the time and possibly even slowing things down for a period of hours or days can help you and your organization maintain a more realistic perspective, maintain a sense of calm, maintain your bearing, and allow you to manage fear.

- If you have an emergency checklist, look at that now.

- If you don't have a checklist, make one now. Don't panic.

- What is your team's top, most pressing priority?

- Get everyone in one room to determine the scope of the problem, and gather as much information as possible.

- Observe, listen, ask questions.

The next time you're faced with a crisis, your first step should be to **hack the clock.**

Task switching and
task saturation are
the number-one
killers of successfully
executing your goals.
—CAREY LOHRENZ

Remember this, my friends: task switching and task saturation are the number-one killers of successfully executing your goals. In fact, the National Business Aviation Association puts task saturation in its top ten threats to business aviation safety,[9] and the phenomenon has contributed to many accidents.

Here's just one example. Recently, four Air Force F-16s were taxiing to the runway, when one plane rear-ended another. The pilot of the first aircraft had stopped on the taxiway to do a standard check of his radar. The second and third aircraft stopped behind him. The fourth aircraft was busy doing aircraft systems checks and failed to realize the plane in front of him had stopped. The offending aircraft received damage totaling more than $2 million; the third aircraft in the formation had almost $600,000 worth of damage. The accident investigation found that there was a breakdown in task prioritization, along with task switching.

The best-trained professionals succumb as well. Air traffic controllers give clearance to airliners to land when an airplane is still on the runway. Surgeons leave instruments in patients at the end of operations. Maintenance crews forget to pass down critical safety information mid-shift and cause gas explosions on oil rigs—like the Piper Alpha disaster of 1988. Even in more everyday ways, we make gaffes and mistakes that may or may not cost us significantly. Maybe you're working on several emails at once and you accidentally refer to your client by the wrong name or hit "send" on a time-sensitive email without attaching an important pdf. And how many times a week do you hear about fender benders where someone was not effectively task switching as they sent a text and ran smack-dab into the car in front of them?

A great deal of these errors could have been prevented if we humans were better at operating in an engaged and focused manner.

When we're task switching, we aren't really fully engaged in anything.

Preventing Task Overload

Task overload is the quickest way to derail solid performance execution. Once we've acknowledged that it *is* a threat and understand *why* we all fall prey to it, then we can take the necessary steps to mitigate it.

TASK OVERLOAD IS THE QUICKEST WAY TO DERAIL SOLID PERFORMANCE EXECUTION.

Countless accidents have occurred in the low-altitude environment because of wrong task priorities. So one of the first and most fundamental things you learn in naval aviation training, particularly when it comes to tricky and risky flights, is the instructional concept of "the Bucket."

The Bucket is a tool in the Navy's Low Altitude Awareness Training used to describe the finite capacity a human pilot has for "input and subsequent action in the low-altitude environment." In other words, it's a visual illustration to help you identify the only acceptable tasks for your brain to complete in times of peak stress and overwhelm.

Within the Naval Bucket are two categories of tasks: (1) Terrain Clearance Tasks and (2) Mission Tasks, which is subdivided into Critical Tasks and Non-Critical Tasks.

Terrain Clearance Tasks (TCT) involves any mental or physical effort needed to avoid the number-one thing you want to avoid when flying a plane: hitting the ground. You can guess that these are higher priority. These are things like control of the aircraft, vector control, altitude control, and time control.

Mission Tasks (MT) encompasses any and all remaining activities required to accomplish your mission—these are lower on the priority scale. Critical MTs are the ones demanding immediate attention, while non-critical MTs are lower priority.

The Bucket looks like this:

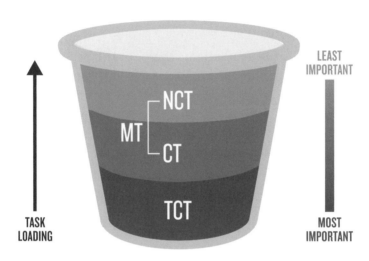

You fill it first with your number-one priority—then whatever room is left of that Bucket you can fill with critical tasks and then non-critical tasks. Remember, your *primary task*, i.e., the most important, will always be first in and last out.

Bottom line? Take the time to identify the most important work you should be focusing on, the work that if you don't do it, you'll "hit the ground."

TCT, CT, NCT.

The Bucket illustrates how to identify when task saturation is occurring and what to prioritize.

BOTTOM LINE? TAKE THE TIME TO IDENTIFY THE MOST IMPORTANT WORK YOU SHOULD BE FOCUSING ON, THE WORK THAT IF YOU DON'T DO IT, YOU'LL "HIT THE GROUND."

As task loading increases, we need to be able to task-shed the less critical items.

Don't get hung up on the acronyms.

In layman's terms: don't try to do everything at once, don't task switch, and don't focus on things that don't matter.

How will we know or recognize when we, or a teammate, are becoming overloaded? In aviation, **overtasking cues** are the signs of psychological and physiological stress that manifest themselves in one or more of the ways listed below:

1. momentary indecision or confusion (feeling of being "behind the aircraft").

2. Wasted movements in the cockpit.

3. Missed tasks and checks.

4. Erratic or inconsistent basic airwork.

5. Loss of, late, or nonstandard verbal response.

6. Loss of overall situational awareness.

It cannot be overemphasized that aircrew need to understand these cues in order to have a frame of reference for recognizing over-tasking and misprioritization of cockpit tasking.

With experience, you'll feel more comfortable recognizing task overload, preparing to prevent it, planning to respond by being intentional about your focus targets, task shedding, and staying focused on your Span of Control.

Use the Bucket to develop the skill to be intentional about what you are focusing on.

THE BUCKET

The Bucket is an effective tool for prioritizing. Think about what is most important to you right now, like a financial or a fitness goal. Think of the importance of each step along that success chain that needs to happen in order to hit that goal.

1. Most important = these go in first.

2. Not as important = put these in second.

3. Nice to have but not 100 percent necessary = these go in third.

Fill the Bucket below, and make some notes regarding what kind of tasks would fall under each category.

1st: _____

_____

_____

_____

_____

2nd: _____

_____

_____

_____

_____

3rd: _____

_____

_____

_____

_____

Seven—Plus or Minus Two

In a postpandemic world, a lot of us will be trying to figure out how to move forward in our personal lives, working from home, leading our teams, saving, maintaining, maybe even growing our businesses. The challenge is that the landscape has changed. Dramatically. And it continues to change.

Data and information are coming at us quickly, and we need to be able to sort and retain what is most important and move forward with courage, tenacity, persistence, and patience.

On the first day of flight school, sitting on top of every desk was a stack of books and manuals over a foot and a half tall. We were told that we would be responsible for knowing everything contained in those books, soup to nuts, in six weeks' time. Otherwise, we would wash out—that is, we wouldn't make it through the program. If we weren't able to drink from the fire hose, this occupation was not for us.

Flight school is similar to med school in that you have to learn, memorize, recite, and understand a mountain of critical information in a very short period of time. And you have to be able to do all of that not only when safely on the ground and under pressure from demanding flight instructors, but you also have to be able to recall, reason, and continue to make effective decisions while you're flying in physically demanding environments.

We used mnemonics—acronyms, rhymes, flashcards, juggling while repeating blocks of information, running while spouting checklists, "chair flying" our flights in our kitchens or living rooms—to help us chunk all the information down into memorable, *actionable* pieces that we could quickly and easily recall.

The challenge was that you had to actually think *and* fly—at the same time. You may scoff at that, thinking it's not that much different from thinking and driving, which isn't so difficult (though even in a car you can cause a lot of damage by daydreaming). But ask any military aviation instructor, and he or she will tell you that more than one supersmart aerospace engineer or rocket scientist has been unable to think, fly, and talk on the radios all at the same time.

In fact, my brother, now a retired military pilot, once had a student that fell into that category. He thought this fella was brilliant (he was an aerospace engineer), funny, and easygoing. In other words, the student seemed like he'd be a perfect person to fly with. On one flight in a superdynamic part of the training maneuver, things got overwhelming in the cockpit, and the plane the student was flying just started drifting. My brother, the instructor, kept saying "You have the controls, [student's name], you have the controls!" After several seconds of nonresponsive behavior, suddenly the student's gloved hands raised up toward the canopy, and he spoke: *"I am Batman … "*

Yup. The flight was done, and so ended another aspiring naval aviator's career.

Even the smartest among us can get so overwhelmed by too much data or information coming at us that maybe internally, with our inside voice, we are saying, "I am Batman … "

So, we need to have a way to **clarify the complex**—then chunk it up into small, specific bites so that we can retain it, during good times and bad, while focusing on our Span of Control.

That's where seven—plus or minus two—comes in.

Back in 1956, George A. Miller, cognitive psychologist at Princeton University, published what would become one of the most renowned papers in his field.

He's responsible for what's known as Miller's Law—a law stating that at any given time, the average human can only hold about seven items in short-term memory. Miller's Law reinforces what the Bucket teaches us: our brain has limits to what it can hold and do at one time. The more you stretch those limits, the more likely you are to crash and burn.

Miller had noticed that no matter what the subject matter was, people were only able to hold on to about seven pieces of new information—"plus or minus two"—so, roughly five to nine things. Whether it was musical notes, letters, words, or digits, participants in his studies would do okay when they had two or three to choose from, but they would start getting confused when the number of choices exceeded six. No matter the test contents, people tended to hit their accuracy limit around seven—plus or minus two.

What's less widely known, though, is Miller's idea of *chunks*. Meaning, you might be able to recall seven digits or letters, but you're also able to recall seven numbers, words, or even phrases. If you "chunk" the information into familiar units, you can remember them as individual items.[10]

Think about the cadence in saying a phone number—a ten-digit number. We tend to group those numbers into smaller groups of numbers—we present them in hyphenated chunks of, say, one and three and three and four. (Say it out loud: 1-412-555-1240—see what I mean?) Or let's say you were given a list of letters: B.U.S.L.A.S.T.C.A.L.L.S.E.E. That's twelve individual characters long—much longer than Miller says you'll be able to remember. But if you remember it instead as *bus, last, call, see*, you'll be able to remember four words and then the individual letters within them.

Newer studies have brought that number down even more, placing the limit at three or four. Modern researchers believe that without chunking, we can really only hold three or four things in our working memory at once.

Which brings me back to *meatball, line up, angle of attack*.

In the cockpit of my Tomcat, I was able to do rapid task switching, from meatball to line up to angle of attack, because *I'd trained to balance those three intertwined elements* of a successful landing, each of which had chunked skills and specific tasks underneath it. Even within the Bucket of our conceptual goals, there are individual tasks with varying levels of priority. I had a mental model.

It's too simplistic to say that all task switching is bad. Indeed, sometimes you have to do it. Task switching can also be harmless when you're doing two tasks, only one of which requires higher functioning of your brain. You're perfectly fine, for example, to listen to an audiobook or podcast while folding laundry or doing the dishes. Your brain can do those chores basically on autopilot.

THE PROBLEM COMES WHEN WE THOUGHTLESSLY TASK SWITCH BECAUSE WE HAVEN'T IDENTIFIED WHAT MATTERS MOST AND HAVEN'T TAKEN AN INVENTORY OF THE ITEMS THAT ARE MOST FIRMLY WITHIN OUR SPAN OF CONTROL.

The problem comes when we thoughtlessly task switch because we haven't identified what matters most and haven't taken an inventory of the items that are most firmly within our Span of Control.

At the end of the day, our brains have limits. *Understanding our limitations* is the only way we can optimize our mental faculties and actually accomplish our goals, dreams, and commitments.

By understanding how our brains function when our schedules, to-do lists, and figurative buckets overflow, we can take immediate and effective strides toward getting closer to the person we've wanted to be but may have lost sight of somewhere along the way.

It's time to take back control—to focus on what we want, dump the unnecessary (and hopefully the heart monitor!), and ditch the patterns that keep us stuck living by default instead of by design.

FOCUS QUESTIONS

- What are the things that often come up and distract you? List them to become more aware of them.

- What are the *most important* things you need to get done this week? Write them down. As per Miller's Law, try grouping them into three or four categories and then focusing on only those three or four each day. If you happen to achieve more than that, great! But don't beat yourself up if you just manage to tackle those three—in fact, celebrate if you do!

- What goes on your don't-do list? Write down some of the things you want to *stop* doing.

Chapter 3

BURNOUT

A s a fighter pilot, I have always had the companions of pressure and stress, starting postcollege in Aviation Officer Candidate School (AOCS) at Naval Air Station Pensacola, Florida, a place affectionately referred to as "the Pressure Cooker."

Pensacola's AOCS started training officer candidates in 1936. Legends like Neil Armstrong, Buzz Aldrin, and John McCain all went through AOCS. Even if you made it through to graduation and earned your commission, only a handful of those who made it to Pensacola's AOCS would eventually go on to earn those prized golden naval aviator wings. And then only an extremely small percentage of those would go on to become aircraft carrier fighter pilots.

We knew we had to earn the right to be there. Every. Single. Day. Our United States Marine Corps drill instructors were finding out who could hack it and who couldn't. Every day, minute by minute under the broiling Florida sun, the drill instructors were, in fact, trying to break us, both physically and psychologically.

Their jobs were difficult: they had to take civilian college graduates and jam four years of what would have been training at the

Naval Academy or an ROTC program into a sixteen-week program, to turn out a commissioned officer ready to lead and succeed in military aviation.

AOCS consisted of four basic challenge areas—academic, military, physical fitness, and swimming. We learned about naval organization, operations, and law; United States sea power; seamanship; naval leadership; engineering; aerodynamics; air navigation; aviation physiology; survival (land and sea), and much more. And on top of all that came a metric shit ton of physical training. This wasn't easy stuff, and we were told over and over of the spectacular attrition rate: around 50 percent of us wouldn't make it through.

The general gist of the training was this: They were finding our pressure points and attempting to exert as much force on those points as possible. They were identifying the people who couldn't work through the physical and mental stress and challenges we would face. They had to uncover who had the tenacity to keep after their objective, no matter what, and who did not.

The USMC (United States Marine Corps) drill instructors used to drive home the importance of attention to detail. God help you if you were the candidate who accidentally left a rifle unsecured while at class, out on a run, or at water survival. The chances were high that you would find all of your stuff—and your roommate's stuff—out on the lawn of the AOCS Battalion buildings. It was even worse when the instructors found a speck of rust or a piece of fuzz or lint clinging to your rifle in a place you didn't even know existed.

But this rigor, the relentless pace and accountability, set the tone for what would be expected of us farther down the road—a much greater level of responsibility than taking care of an old, used weapon. In order to survive in naval aviation, you absolutely have to pay meticulous attention to detail, *especially* when operating under extraordinarily difficult circumstances.

Much of what we were required to do wasn't glamorous or "energizing." It was hard, dangerous work that required both the motivation and the discipline to keep going long past the point of "feeling like it."

It was the best possible training for what lay ahead. All of it was aimed at developing the instincts and discipline to remain focused on what mattered, to be able to pay attention to detail under extreme circumstances, to rely on teamwork, trust, and mutual support. You had to always lead by example, regardless of rank, title, or position, and to absorb the blows of chaos and uncertainty—to stay flexible, adapt, and overcome any scenario they concocted. All of that was necessary, no matter whether you were flying at Mach two with your hair on fire or flying a helicopter at night through the moonless mountains of Afghanistan.

By focusing on our individual and collective pressure points, our training was essentially testing our capacity to avoid breakdown.

When I work with executives and managers across every industry, I often hear stories about them or their teammates feeling as though they're teetering on the edge of a breakdown, more commonly called burnout, from extreme stress. And too often I hear clients and organizations stating that their goal is to *eliminate* stress. In fact, eliminating all stress should *not* be the goal, though I understand the need to avoid that product of extreme stress known as burnout. Stress will always be there if you are striving to achieve more, if you are operating at the edges of the envelope. And likely, it'll be there even if you aren't doing those things!

Midpandemic, it's probably safe to say we can all agree that the

ELIMINATING ALL STRESS SHOULD *NOT* BE THE GOAL.

goal is to do everything possible to mitigate chronic or acute stress: we're working out, eating lots of fruits and vegetables, doing mindfulness training, thinking positively, meditating, you name it.

The problem is that those things aren't working for a lot of people. Or they're not working well enough by themselves, and we are losing talented teammates.

Learning how to absorb the blows and harness your adrenaline to focus on your Span of Control can help when it comes to countering overwhelming stress. If you can do that? You've got a shot.

Clinically, burnout is *not* classified as a medical condition. It is defined as an occupational phenomenon caused by chronic workplace stress. The word *burnout* was first coined as a technical term by Herbert Freudenberger in 1975 and was defined by three main components:

- feelings of energy depletion or exhaustion,

- increased mental distance from one's job, or feelings of negativity and cynicism related to one's job, and

- reduced professional efficacy or feeling a low sense of professional accomplishment.

We tend to believe burnout happens because of overwork, long hours, or burning the candle at both ends. But in reality, the majority of burnout cases—as the definition suggests—aren't simply the result of a crushing lack of sleep or too many tasks. They're about feeling

- unsupported,

- undervalued,

- disconnected, or even

- unsafe, whether psychologically or physically.

And any perceived threat of harm simply escalates these feelings. Ultimately, burnout comes down to a lack of support and

Ultimately, burnout comes down to a lack of support and empathy from those around us—and that, my friends, amounts to a leadership problem.

—CAREY LOHRENZ

empathy from those around us—and that, my friends, amounts to a leadership problem. Our colleagues and teammates and direct reports are not only suffering from stress but also from a kind of morale injury.

We have been seeing symptoms of burnout in those who are engaged in frontline activities: healthcare workers, emergency response personnel, grocery and supply chain workers, postal workers, and military members. When it comes to those frontline workers, they want to do their jobs with compassion and care, but they simply don't have the tools or resources to serve everyone in need. That leads to feelings of helplessness and overwhelm.

Worse yet?

Stress skyrockets when we are on the same team but competing for a limited number of resources.

Being a leader means you must have and display the ability to understand, support, and provide both psychological and physical safety to those you lead: your teammates, your employees, your constituents, your community, your family, and even yourself.

Fight, Flight, Freeze ... or Autopilot

We've all heard about the typical responses to overwhelm, exhaustion, and stress:

- *fight*—you aggressively meet the thing that is frustrating you head-on to overcome it,

- *flight*—you quickly move away from the thing that is causing all the stress, or

- *freeze*—you become paralyzed and unable to make any necessary moves toward a solution.

But there is a fourth option, often overlooked and sometimes maligned: autopilot.

Autopilot is a piece of technology that, once programmed, steers a plane without human interference. You can input settings like speed and altitude, and the autopilot will maintain those settings for as long as the plane has fuel in its tank. Autopilot systems free up the human pilot to fly the plane without compromising focus, thus ruling out countless forms of human error.

When we talk about autopilot in terms of our human capacities—the functions we can rely on because they are such ingrained habits in us—we recognize that shifting to autopilot can sometimes be a great asset. This is particularly true in high-workload environments, where you instinctively rely on your training and can go through the motions with little attentional energy.

Autopilot is the perfect pilot—except, of course, if there is a flock of ducks coming in hot. Or a massive storm showing up on the radar. Or if utilizing autopilot leads to complacency, because everything feels ops normal.

Sure, the autopilot has plenty of warnings—ringing bells, blinking lights—but it's not going to *do* anything on its own about whatever caused those bells and lights to activate in the first place. Left unattended, the autopilot will result in a crash-and-burn moment.

If you haven't already, you will find yourself in a situation sooner or later where you are exhausted, you are maxed out, you feel as though you've run out of options. You may even be functioning on autopilot, going through the motions of your days without really being present or actively engaged.

It's like when you drive home only to step out of your car and barely remember anything about your commute.

Honestly, it's incredible to think of everything that's going on in your brain as you make that drive. Your brain is keeping your lungs breathing, blood moving, heart pumping. It's allowing you to see the lanes, smell the open road, and move the steering wheel. It's automatically retaining the rules of the road while also maintaining that stream of consciousness. (*Can't believe what happened at work today … We need to fill that board seat … Gosh, I really need to get a new vacuum cleaner … I think we should probably hire another cyber security expert … I wonder how Sarah is doing … *). That's a lot of things to juggle at once, and yet you do it seamlessly on a daily basis.

The fact that we are creatures of habit and routine isn't necessarily a bad thing. It actually serves us well at times. The scientific community suggests that we make about 35,000 decisions each day—our brain couldn't possibly process at the same level every single thing we do. That means, whenever it is able, your brain will kick into an automatic decision-making mode to save mental energy and to free up your conscious mind to work on particularly demanding or important things. If we were to be stimulated and aware of every single thing that is happening around us at any given moment … well, we'd likely implode. This automatic feature in our brains makes life a hell of a lot easier.

AUTOPILOT IS AN INCREDIBLE EVOLUTIONARY MIRACLE, BUT IT'S ALSO GOT THE POTENTIAL TO LEAD TO WILDLY UNPRODUCTIVE AND UNFULFILLING ACTIVITY.

Autopilot is an incredible evolutionary miracle, but it's also got the potential to lead to wildly unproductive and unfulfilling activity. To function on autopilot is to lack focus and clarity, only accomplishing the automized mundanities of your day-to-day. It's the reason you're bummed out, overwhelmed, overworked, and feel like you have lost control.

A study done by Harvard University psychologists Matthew Killingsworth and Daniel Gilbert, author of *Stumbling on Happiness*, revealed that the average person spends 47 percent of their waking hours doing what they call *mind wandering*, which is essentially just your thoughts on autopilot.

You heard that right: 47 percent. That's nearly *half of our lives,* people!

When that automatic feature starts slipping into more and more areas of your life—especially ones that need more conscious consideration, it comes at a cost. It can lead you to feeling that you've run out of options.

The important question to ask is this: Have you really?

One fall afternoon several years ago, one of my former flight school classmates, Capt. Scott "Fface" Slater, a USMC F/A-18 fighter pilot, launched off the USS *Nimitz* on what he believed to be a "routine" mission. (The hair should already be standing on the back of your neck here, because *nothing* is ever "routine" when launching off an aircraft carrier loaded with weapons).

The flight op began just like any other: the preflight planning and briefing were normal, the walk to the jet normal, the prelaunch inspection of the fully loaded-out airplane purportedly normal, and the launch off the carrier incident-free, so "normal."

He and his wingman continued on their mission, accomplishing various aggressive tasks and maneuvers, and everything was still OK. Then it was time to land.

Now, for those of you unfamiliar with flight and aircraft carrier operations, there are a few idiosyncrasies that are important to note. We have to land within a very specific weight range (i.e., not too heavy) so as not to overstress the airplane or the aircraft carrier arresting gear equipment (i.e., the cables that are laid across the landing area that your tailhook snags to stop you). When you're loaded with weapons, you're heavier than normal, so you can't land with much fuel. And it can get dicey. (For the super-detail-oriented folks, I'll include a quick note that the F/A-18 Hornet burns around six hundred pounds of fuel making just one circle around a daytime carrier landing pattern. Keep that in mind.)

Fface and his wingman came roaring into the break overhead the aircraft carrier at about five hundred knots; it was a sunny day, blue sky, the perfect time for a max-performance overhead approach.

As Fface rolled into the abeam position, decelerating through 250 knots, he dropped the gear handle to lower the landing gear. Only a handful of seconds away from landing, he realized immediately there was a problem: unbeknownst to Fface, earlier in flight a failed D-ring had sheared the hydraulic lines, and all the hydraulic fluid leaked out and was trapped in the wheel well. When the landing gear doors opened, the hydraulic fluid immediately flew out of the bottom of the aircraft and into the engines.

Billows of gray smoke filled the cockpit, and Fface was momentarily blinded by the smoke. Any aviator worth his or her salt knows by heart every nook, cranny, and circuit breaker in their airplane precisely for when these exact scenarios arise. We've spent countless hours training doing the mundane, disciplined work required to memorize every square inch by touch. So with his eyes closed and watering, Fface was able to quickly work through his memorized checklist to clear the smoke from the cockpit and get back to one of our mantras: "Aviate. Navigate. Communicate." Fly the jet. Keep it pointed in the right direction. Let people know what is going on.

Every pilot relies on relentless preparation, effective checklists, maintaining their composure, staying calm under pressure, and retaining the ability to execute and compartmentalize effectively— i.e., knowing what is within our Span of Control—to get us through these dangerous situations. Working through his checklists and with a radio assist from his wingman, Wolfy (yup, real callsign and another flight school classmate), Fface was able to successfully get the main landing gear down—but not the nose gear. This is not good for a carrier-based operation.

There was no other place to land than the aircraft carrier. No divert airfield. No cushy ten-thousand-foot landing strip to ease down onto. The option to eject was discussed, as was rigging the barricade.

The conclusion: they had to rig the barricade. The crew of the USS *Nimitz* worked as quickly as they could to raise across the aircraft carrier deck what looks similar to a big tennis court net. By this time, Fface was down to about three hundred pounds of fuel. Fumes.

Focusing on nothing but meatball, line up, angle of attack, the only things within his Span of Control, he knew he had one shot.

The goal: fight to fly a perfect pass—on speed, on glide slope, and perfect line up right into that net.

Meatball. Line up. Angle of attack.

Under extreme pressure, by focusing on what mattered most, executing the emergency plan, communicating clearly, and disregarding all other distractions, they successfully "caught the fighter in the tennis net." And *that* is the amazing story of the *first* F/A-18 barricade in the history of naval aviation.

Capt. Scott "Fface" Slater went on to earn an MBA from Vanderbilt, to work in private wealth management, to buy and sell several companies, and to fly for a major airline. When we chatted about his reflections on that fateful day, for which he was awarded an Air Medal, he said this: "Leadership during challenging times is the key. We must personally be technically and tactically proficient. That requires years of experience. Anyone can be the captain of the ship on a calm day. It's what the skipper does or does not do in the midst of the storm that determines whether the ship, the team, or the company lives or dies."

Fface offers an answer to that earlier question: *Have you really run out of options?* Technical and tactical proficiency and preparation can help us see and take advantage of options even in the midst of a crisis situation. The important thing is not to wait for a crisis to hit to discover how you, or your team, will adapt to a dangerous or changing situation. Because you rarely see it coming.

> ## THE IMPORTANT THING IS NOT TO WAIT FOR A CRISIS TO HIT TO DISCOVER HOW YOU, OR YOUR TEAM, WILL ADAPT TO A DANGEROUS OR CHANGING SITUATION. BECAUSE YOU RARELY SEE IT COMING.

At the end of the day, if one of us is in trouble, all of us could be in trouble. Our Span of Control ultimately involves elements of teamwork, trust, and mutual support. Recognizing and addressing the challenges in ourselves as much as in others enables us to lead through change, uncertainty, and complexity—all with confidence and integrity. Understanding how we respond to stress, how our teammates respond to stress, and then being intentional about choosing a different response or reaction is critical to successfully navigating the speed of change and leading ourselves and our teams through challenging times.

Recognizing Burnout

No one really *plans* for burnout or thinks much about how to recognize its symptoms before they take over. But maybe we should, because burnout comes for all of us eventually.

In Navy training, the road to burnout is paved with those "over-tasking cues" or signs of psychological stress that we reviewed in chapter 2: the momentary indecision or confusion, wasted movements, missed tasks, nonstandard verbal responses, and loss of situational awareness.

The *Low Altitude Training Manual* states "It cannot be overemphasized that aircrew need to understand these cues in order to have a frame of reference for recognizing overtasking and mis-prioritization of cockpit tasking."

Similar symptoms are recognizable in the business arena too. In my experience, whether I'm working with industrial teams, hospital teams, business owners, high-performing athletes, or salespeople, the four major telltale symptoms of dangerous task overload and the approach of burnout—for pilots, professionals, and just normal people doing everyday things—are surprisingly subtle and easy to miss.

They are: shutting down, compartmentalizing, channelizing, and overindulging or escaping into our coping mechanisms.

SHUTTING DOWN

In the face of a seemingly impossible situation, you simply stop functioning. We've all worked with people who have reached this stage; you've seen their arms go up in the air as they yell, "I've had it! I'm done!" Or you've seen others completely close off and get unusually quiet.

Now, I'm not a yeller, but when I get overwhelmed, I mean *really* overwhelmed, I tend to get quieter, calmer—demeanor-wise anyway. (On the inside, my hamster wheels are spinning at Mach 2.) I'm just trying to manage everything without causing any additional agitation or drama. Unfortunately, that can look like apathy to some people, or worse, they can fail to see that I am struggling at all. And that can lead to disasters.

COMPARTMENTALIZING

When you compartmentalize, you shut down certain parts of the brain in an attempt to focus on just one thing at a time. By ignoring, denying, or repressing certain things, however, you are missing the big picture. You might skip tasks, and your work may become erratic and inconsistent.

CHANNELIZING

When you channelize, you focus on one thing to the total exclusion of all others; it's like having tunnel vision. Pilots who are channelizing their attention may miss radio calls, fail to see other airplanes, or be in the midst of target fixation, which typically happens when a pilot is nose-down, pointed toward the ground, on a diving target run at 500 knots. He or she is focused—too focused—and may forget to actually fly the jet. With eyes on the target, the pilot flies the jet straight at it—and straight into the ground. That's called "dying relaxed." We can all sometimes have such a tight focus on the task at hand that, oftentimes to our peril, we ignore incoming phone calls or repeated texts that may be important and time sensitive.

OVERINDULGING COPING MECHANISMS

The word *coping* suggests all good things, but do you ever notice when things fall apart and life goes haywire, we tend to overindulge in the things that comfort us? In March 2020, as COVID-19 was first brought to our attention in the US and quickly escalated into worldwide calls for self-quarantine, the number of coping-driven behaviors increased dramatically. For instance, television streaming increased 85 percent in the US.[11] Of course, this could be explained in part by the fact that millions of Americans had way more time on their hands (I watched *Ozark* season three for the *third* time, *Game of Thrones* for the fourth, and all the Jason Bourne movies again), but it also shows that we dramatically increase our coping mechanisms when chaos and uncertainty strike.

Some of us reach for another glass of wine (in March 2020, wine sales increased by 66 percent),[12] while others overindulge in comfort food (pastry sales jumped by 18 percent the first week of March alone).[13] Still others escape with endless social media scrolling. No shame here, but how often do we use the same ol' mechanisms for moments that are way less debilitating than a colossal epidemic?

Remember that the true definition of coping involves dealing *effectively* with something difficult. Sometimes that *can* totally be decompressing with your favorite rerun and momentarily distracting yourself if you are reaching peak overwhelm. Heck, in the first four months of the pandemic and in between nonstop Zoom calls, I was making different kinds of bread every single day: sourdough, French bread, Dutch oven, with a starter, without a starter, overnight rise, fast-rise, rosemary/olive oil, sea salt, banana, pumpkin—you name it, I baked it.

But eventually, I was going to have to save the crime drama and bread baking for another day. We all have to look out for signs that we might be tangling up what is within our Span of Control with procrastinating, or even numbing, as we try to handle anxiety and stress. Everyone is wired differently. The key is to understand how you and your teammates, your colleagues, and your family are wired—how you and they respond to stress and overwhelm.

THE KEY IS TO UNDERSTAND HOW YOU AND YOUR TEAMMATES, YOUR COLLEAGUES, AND YOUR FAMILY ARE WIRED— HOW YOU AND THEY RESPOND TO STRESS AND OVERWHELM.

Shutting down, compartmentalizing, channelizing, and over-indulging your coping or escaping mechanisms—even turning to autopilot for some relief—all of these things happen when your brain decides that you are too small to fight or too weak to flee, that the problems you are facing outweigh your capability to overcome them. These are evolutionary reactions.

Of course, there are times in life where the bad news is so overwhelming and insurmountable that just keeping your head above water is an achievement. Survival is necessary! The key is to recognize the difference between those most difficult moments or life-altering events and the ones where we could do more than just survive each day.

Remember this, friends: you can do anything, but you can't do everything. Not all at the same time, anyway ...

Being on the lookout for signs of distress—in yourself and others—is the first step toward being able to address that distress. Once you understand *why* we are prone to making mistakes in our execution, particularly under stressful conditions, and can spot when task overload and burnout are happening, the next step is to mitigate the risks. Alleviating distress is a process that begins with subtle shifts in mindset and yields decisive and purposeful action in the direction of our goals.

FOCUS QUESTIONS

- Which signs of burnout do you notice in yourself, your family, your teams?

- Which of the things that you do on autopilot would you like to be more fully engaged and present for?

- Is there a level of stress that you find helpful or invigorating?

PART II
MINDSET MATTERS

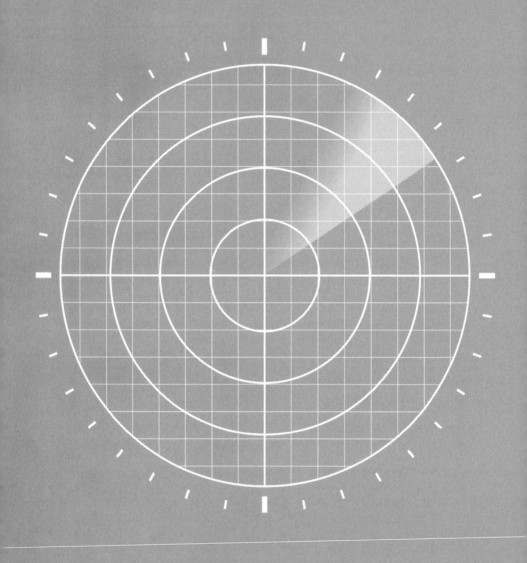

Chapter 4

FIGHT FOR PURPOSE

How can you fly your plane with an empty fuel tank? Or when autopilot's typical soul-sucking solution won't do the trick? What do you do when you're feeling drained, uninspired, or just plain *meh*?

Given that I'm a fighter pilot, you can probably guess what I am going to tell you to do.

You fight. You fight like hell for the life you want. You fight for purpose. And you fight for focus.

During that period of peak burnout in my life, I had to start small. I had to first let some things go, to simplify and focus on what mattered most.

Business proposals were launched when they were done, not agonized over until they were "perfect." For short-notice house showings, I shoved laundry into the dryer, folded or not, or simply took it out and launched it in the back of my car in a laundry basket. *Winning.* I didn't attend every PTA meeting, especially those last-minute ones that could've been handled via email. (Sorry not sorry, fellow PTA board members.) I *did* attend every business board meeting, because those you can't miss.

At home, I started picking my battles. I focused on what was *reasonably* within my Span of Control. If my four-year-old insisted on wearing a tutu over her leopard pants for the third day in a row? Fine. As long as she had a clean shirt and clean undies, you do you, girl.

Instead of making homemade cookies every single time the room mom asked, I bought construction paper and gift cards for the teachers. Craft away, kids, craft away.

I had to be OK with sometimes letting go of the idea instilled in me since I was a little girl that fifteen minutes early was on time, on time was late, and late was unacceptable. When your three-year-old pukes all over themselves while wearing a dinosaur costume, soaking themselves and the car seat straps? Well, you're going to have to grab some Wet Wipes and breathe—because you're about to be late.

There are many ways to fight for purpose. They include:

- flexibility,

- focusing on facts over fear,

- feeling your feelings, and

- facing your failures head-on.

> I GAVE UP FEELING LIKE I HAD TO BE ABLE TO DO EVERYTHING RIGHT. I HAD TO GIVE UP *RIGHT* FOR *RIGHT FOR THE MOMENT.*

These are all proactive and *meaningful* reactions to uncertainty and overwhelm.

I gave up feeling like I had to be able to do everything right. I had to give up *right* for *right for the moment.*

I was able to get done what needed to be done and let go of everything I couldn't. I accepted that certain things were within my Span of Control and others weren't. It was painful at times, but not as painful as trying to do *everything* ... and ending up doing nothing.

It was a great lesson learned and one I've carried forward as I continued to grow my business and raise four kids.

There will be trade-offs on your journey, as there were on mine.

There were countless times people told me I needed to "go big" with my business, "scale for greater impact—now!" But I've stayed clear on my purpose and my priorities. Even right now I have a team the size that feels manageable for me; we are touching hundreds of thousands of people a year, and I'm 100 percent there for my kids as well. I actively block off time on my calendar for those dates that I will not compromise on, and I say "no" to those events that won't serve my family well. It's a choice. And I'm grateful to have the choice.

But it's also about being very clear about what my purpose is and what success looks like *for me, and I work hard at it.*

"Too much" certainly isn't the only way to burn out. "Too little" is equally draining. If you aren't living with purpose fueling you, it's pretty easy to get burned out on the monotony of the day-to-day. What should be meaningful starts to feel mundane.

That's one of the best things about purpose: it's burnout's kryptonite. When you are actively pursuing your purpose, it can help keep burnout at bay. A sense of purpose is the single most important factor in your success, especially during times of overwhelm and uncertainty.

That's true as much for teams as for individuals. On the aircraft carrier, one of the most dangerous industrial worksites in the world, it was imperative that we all shared clarity of vision and purpose, we all knew what success looked like, and we understood the role we each played in making it a reality. Setting and sustaining that vision was a matter of leadership empowering the team to achieve high performance, to find and hold to their purpose.

In aviation, just as in business and at work, we may not have

That's one of the best things about purpose: it's burnout's kryptonite. When you are actively pursuing your purpose, it can help keep burnout at bay. A sense of purpose is the single most important factor in your success, especially during times of overwhelm and uncertainty.

—CAREY LOHRENZ

chosen one another as teammates, but we can all get focused on doing one thing and doing it well. Whether you lead a group of five or 150,000, it's imperative that you, as a leader, step up and provide the vision that empowers your team. An inspiring vision is the fuel that allows us all to attain uncommon results.

ID THREE THINGS, DO ONE THING

Three Things

In the morning before you turn on your phone, open up your laptop, or have that first cup of coffee or tea, do this: grab your stash of large Post-it Notes and a fat Sharpie marker. Start by writing down your top three things to focus on for the day.

You don't get five to seven; I don't care how important you think your role is.

Write down three. This is hard work, don't kid yourself.

These are your top three things—those that will move your performance needle the most, not a laundry list of things you can easily check off.

Put that Post-it Note where you will see it most—on your laptop, back of your phone, desktop monitor, dashboard ... wherever you're going to see that bad boy fifteen, thirty, forty times a day.

One Thing

A good way to build your powers of concentration is to practice committing 100 percent to whatever you're doing in the moment. Do *one thing* at a time—not two or three or four, not one active thing and one passive thing.

One thing.

If you're in a meeting, put your phone away and be present. If you're writing a speech on the laptop, turn off the Wi-Fi signal so you won't be tempted to browse. If you're watching a new TV show, really watch it—don't scroll Instagram, Facebook, or TikTok.

When you build your focus muscles by doing one thing, you'll notice that your capacity to focus bleeds over into other areas of your life. You'll fall into the trap of task switching much less often, and you'll get a lot better at concentrating on what matters most.

Fight for Joy

One of the top amplifiers of burnout—both professionally and personally—is the feeling of a lack of control. Span of Control tells us that while not everything is within our ability to change, there are certainly things that are, and *those* are the ones worth actively pursuing. The idea of fighting for joy is one of the number-one *actions* that is always within your Span of Control.

To fight for your joy means to tap back into what you love or find even one aspect of your job, your sport, your hobby that once brought—or might bring—you delight. Why did you start it to begin with? Why did you get involved? Sometimes we focus so hard on achieving a goal that once we've reached it, we feel lost and empty. A what-the-hell-is-the-point? feeling can envelop us. It's during those times that you've got to dig deep to find the parts of your life you love and even remind yourself "**I *get* to do this.**"

How do you stay truly engaged? What tools are we armed with in our fight for joy?

GRATITUDE

This wouldn't be a book on leadership and self-development if I didn't mention the idea of gratitude, right? I get it. You know intellectually that gratitude is good for you, and undoubtedly, every time someone reminds you to be grateful, you get a twinge of guilt (perhaps mixed with a dash of annoyance/resentment) for not feeling thankful all the time. It's hard. But science backs it up. Several studies have confirmed that gratitude improves physical, emotional, and mental health by combating stress, anxiety, and burnout.[14]

There is a process called habituation where your brain filters out the ordinary happenings that don't change every day, whether it's your dishwasher running or the rush of your car engine starting. While habituation is an efficient use of your brain's neural resources, it causes a lot of the good that's around us all the time to go unnoticed.[15]

This means we have to actively attend to what we are grateful for and keep a record of it.

Whether it's better sleep, less sickness, or greater happiness, a plethora of studies have traced a range of impressive benefits to the simple act of writing down the things for which we're grateful. In most of these studies, people are instructed to write down five things, in just one line each. Those things can range from the mundane ("waking up in the morning") to new and exciting ("getting a new house") to the timeless ("music"). Below, write down five things you are grateful for today. Take your time. Think about what your life would be without certain things, and think of the things that bring you deep joy.

1. _____

2. _____

3. _____

4. _____

5. _____

LIFETIME LEARNING

Continuous learning and expanding of horizons are key to staying curious and engaged, which is key to staying motivated and fulfilled. So make it a habit. What is that bit of learning you've put on the back burner? Learn Mandarin? Learn to crochet? Read all the great literary classics? Fly a plane? Bake the perfect chocolate soufflé?

Write it down here: _____

_____

_____

_____

And now do one thing—just *one* thing—right now that holds you accountable to what you've chosen to learn. I'm serious—put this book down for a second (or hit pause on your Audible) and do the darn thing. Sign up for lessons. Order the book. Schedule a meeting. Buy the ingredients. TAKE ACTION.

TECHNOLOGY DETOX

Remember this: we are not chained to our devices! Stop the social media doomscrolling. Turn your notifications off. Stop automatically reacting at every ding and ring like Pavlov's dog. It's life-sucking. I know we've all got busy work schedules and family and friends who depend on us, so I get that maybe a full-on technology detox may not be possible for everyone at any ol' time. Here are a couple of baby steps to get those darn distractors out of your line of sight:

- Don't look at your phone for an hour before you go to bed. There's a large body of research that shows using your phone/tablet at night exposes you to blue light, which disrupts your deep REM sleep. This means even if you're trying to get a little more sleep, it won't be high quality.[16]

- Pay attention and internally note every time you feel the impulse to check your phone. When you notice that impulse, ask yourself, "Am I checking out of habit?" and "Is it necessary to check right now?" If it's not necessary, put your phone away.

- Refrain from using your cell phone when interacting with people. This, of course, means when you're out to dinner with family but also when you are ordering coffee from the barista.

- Go tech-free on your next vacation. This may take some planning, but lest we forget, until the last twenty years, it was also the norm.

- Don't hold your phone in your hand or keep it in your pocket when it's not in use. Put it farther away—in your bag or on the counter—and only look at it when you have to.

- Do something in the real world that you would typically do online—for example, get coffee with a friend instead of texting back and forth, or shop local to buy a magazine or a book instead of ordering it on Amazon or reading an article online.[17]

EXERCISE

Let's talk about that body of yours. We probably all know this by now, but exercise is not just about how you look—it's about how you *feel*.

Many people in senior leadership positions often overlook taking care of their own physical health. Some industry leaders fare better than others, but there is room for improvement. Your team and your organization's health depend on you to be in fighting shape both mentally and physically.

Dr. Bruce Rabin, medical director of the Healthy Lifestyle Program at the University of Pittsburgh Medical Center, says that increased oxygen flow to the brain can quickly and effectively reduce stress, and the best way to increase oxygen flow is good ol' fashioned, blood-pumping exercise.

The Stress Institute, an educational and training firm that focuses on understanding and relieving the effects of stress, notes that "Exercise delivers oxygen to the brain, vital organs and muscles immediately and produces endorphins that soothe your mind, body and soul."[18]

Regular aerobic exercise is also the fastest way to reduce the stress hormones adrenaline and cortisol. This in turn brings calm, improves your ability to focus, and helps counter depression.

(Oh, and if you're in a pinch, laughter really is the best fast-acting medicine! It's a classic way to get oxygen flowing quickly.)

SLEEP

Life on board an aircraft carrier can be exhausting. There are no set work hours; the ship operates nonstop—twenty-four hours a day, seven days a week. And when we pilots are not flying, we still have to do our day jobs as maintenance officers, educational services officers, training officers, safety officers, operations officers, and administrative officers.

Sometimes it seems there aren't enough hours in the day to cover all our responsibilities. Furthermore, fighter pilots stand combat alert watches. When I would stand an Alert 5, for example, I was required for the duration of the four-hour watch to be strapped into my jet, with all of the starting equipment hooked up, and actually sitting on the catapult, ready for a speedy launch within five minutes.

Always being "on" is energy consuming.

Beyond those responsibilities, our missions were constantly changing. In a matter of minutes, we could go from screaming low across the California desert at speeds illegal in other parts of the country, trying to avoid adversary aircraft, to landing on a bobbing and pitching carrier deck in the ocean. Some missions we practiced dropping bombs; others were spent honing sophisticated reconnaissance capabilities. We would fly as much as flight operations would allow, some months more than others. It was a feast-or-famine cycle.

It was exhilarating, but it could take its toll on your sleep schedule.

Leaders, check on your people. And check your own sleep habits. You can't always control your operation's tempo, but you cannot ask yourself or your people to be operating continuously in a state of sleep deprivation. Do not dismiss the overall impact quality sleep has on your health and your ability to perform well, make good decisions, and focus on what matters. Sleep does more than just get your day off on the right foot. Lack of sleep has a profound impact on your ability to cope and maintain resiliency, and it turns out that sleeplessness and stress go hand in hand.

> YOU CAN'T ALWAYS CONTROL YOUR OPERATION'S TEMPO, BUT YOU CANNOT ASK YOURSELF OR YOUR PEOPLE TO BE OPERATING CONTINUOUSLY IN A STATE OF SLEEP DEPRIVATION.

Ironically, it's fairly cyclical: Too much stress can cause you to have a bad sleep, leading to mental and physical health issues like poor decision-making, nonstop overthinking, weight gain, chronic depression, and high blood pressure. These can, in turn, cause stress in daily life, poor sleep at night, poor decision-making, nonstop overthinking, weight gain, and chronic depression.

You know already that there have been periods of my life where

I would literally have given my left arm to be able to get one night of good sleep. I'm not alone. According to the National Center on sleep disorders research, forty million Americans struggle with some kind of sleep disorder.[19] Although there are no foolproof techniques for falling asleep when you want to, there are some classic tips like making sure your room is dark, quiet, and at a comfortable temperature; avoid eating or drinking too close to bedtime; take a relaxing warm bath or hot shower right before you head to bed; and you already know the ones about putting away your phones and other tech devices at least an hour before.

Remember, too, that it's counterproductive to try to fall asleep when you're feeling restless or obsessed with stressful thoughts. If that's the case, get up, move to a different room, and try to bore yourself with something dull (not on your phone!). Only when you start feeling drowsy should you go back to bed and try again.[20]

In the end, you can't avoid the stress, chaos, pressure, and uncertainty that comes with life, but you can prepare for it and combat it with intentional choices about your everyday activities. You can and should say "no" to things if they are not within your Span of Control—and if you're running low on fuel, see how you can fill your tank so that you can fight burnout and win.

FOCUS QUESTIONS

- How full is your fuel tank? If it's feeling like it's on empty, ask yourself: When is the last time you got a good night's sleep? When is the last time you had a good sweaty workout?

- Is there anything on your to-do list that is intended to be enjoyable, but because it is something you feel like you have to do, it isn't fun anymore?

- When is the last time you celebrated something small and just had some good fun?

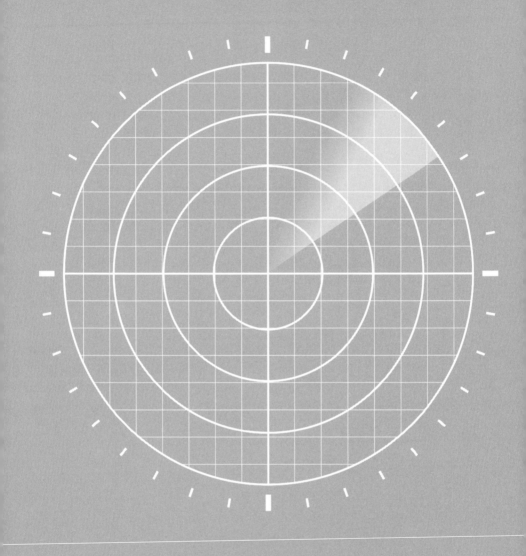

Chapter 5

STAY ROOTED IN REALITY

As you know from the introduction, 2018 was at times a brutal year for me. 2018 was also my Year of Fighting for Joy.

In the space of less than a year, I lost my father-in-law, a much-loved uncle, an aunt, and then my mom, who passed away quite suddenly after succumbing to stage four lung cancer that went undiagnosed and misdiagnosed until just two weeks before her death.

After losing our dad to a patient safety mishap, this was yet another gutting blow for me and my brother.

The two of us were left to handle all the details of managing what was left. We were 1,600 miles away from our own homes and families, trying to get on conference calls, run businesses, and stay connected with our own kids—all while attempting to manage our grief, anger, and frustration at the missed diagnosis. We were sorting through emotions, accounts, finding passwords, tripping over memories, wading through forty-five years of pictures and all the rest of our mom and dad's stuff.

And because of both of our professional commitments and travel schedules, we only had a small window to do it all in. There was no time for collapse. It felt like there was barely a moment to reminisce. We had work to do.

We were trying to keep moving forward, but our distress was just below the spillover point.

On more than one occasion when my brother could tell I was about to completely fall apart, he would simply repeat, "Don't circle the drain, don't circle the drain." I was barely hanging on, my heart broken. And I was tired. In a three-and-a-half-month span, I think I spent a total of three nights in my own bed, between work, travel, and being at the hospital with my mom.

None of this is particularly "special." People have endured worse than I have and made greater sacrifices, no doubt.

This isn't a comparison contest.

Life is hard. Harder at times than others, but whoooeee. 2018 felt like one concrete block to the face after another.

I was fighting the uncertainty and the crumble. Fighting to stay strong for others. Fighting red tape and flawed systems. Fighting the sorrow. Fighting to bounce back. Fighting what felt like never-ending challenges. Fighting for my joy and light, and to give that light to others who needed it more than I did.

Which is why it may be surprising that, even layered in all its heartache, 2018 was also a year of feeling immense gratitude.

I was thankful for my family, who showed up and stayed during the darkest of times, when hope was slipping through our fingers like water. For my kids' countless FaceTime calls.

I felt gratitude for friends who knew that my quiet had nothing to do with them and everything to do with self-preservation.

I felt gratitude for the flight attendant who on what (unbe-knownst to me) would be my final flight to see my mom alive, with a simple head nod and touch to my shoulder, showed enormous com-passion and acknowledgment as so many tears poured silently down my cheeks—clearly no match for my little stack of Delta single-ply napkins.

I felt gratitude for the hugs, the voicemails, the emails, the texts, and especially the NSFW memes. Because laughter isn't always the cure, but it sure is a helluva bridge to hope.

I felt gratitude for the best professional year of my career—doing 107 events across the country and internationally, with only one client event missed. (A shoutout here to the Verizon leadership team, the crew in blue, and the AV pros. You know who you are. Your kindness and compassion and energy will always be remembered. Twenty-six events together, you're family.)

I felt gratitude for my teammates at SpeakersOffice and my speaker bureau partners who made that year possible and who are as equally committed to success as I am.

I felt gratitude for my clients who have become friends. Who trusted me with their teams, their stories, their challenges, and their journeys. We achieved some really big things that year, and I couldn't have been prouder of the work we did.

I also felt gratitude for the clarity that grief can bring and the understanding that each day is both a gift and a challenge ... for resilience ... the ability, the grit to withstand all sorts of pressures ... and for adversity.

Yes, I felt grateful for adversity, and not only because it is not going away anytime soon.

Crucible moments

Let's be honest. History tells us that there is almost nothing new under the sun and that bad things are going to happen to us. Usually, the big stuff hits us out of the blue—a job loss, the death of a loved one, a permanent disability, a miscarriage, a swift economic downturn. These things come from seemingly nowhere, and they can change everything. I call these life-altering moments "crucibles" in that they can define your character, for better or for worse. What most people don't realize is that how you handle your crucibles is the greatest predictor of long-term success.

ADVERSITY INTRODUCES YOU TO YOURSELF.

Adversity introduces you to yourself. How you react—how you respond when the shit hits the fan or when grief envelopes you—can determine whether you survive and thrive or let circumstances destroy you.

Being resilient takes constant positive *action* to bounce back from hardship and rebound from adversity. It takes the ability to withstand, recover, adapt, and grow in the face of stressors and changing demands. Resilience is what you need when everything blows up in your face—when it feels as though you were just hit by a meteor.

One thing that is always (and I mean *always*) within your Span of Control is your mindset.

As humans, **our mindset is our superpower.** We have a keen ability to reconstruct narratives, to redefine moments, and, most important, to learn from them. While your mindset is one of the most difficult things to master, it is indeed the most empowering tool in your pursuit to take back control of your life, your business, or your future.

The benefits of a resilient mindset are, of course, not just personal.

Understanding your own responses along with your teammates' reactions to grief, loss, trauma, and change will be critical to your ability to lead others through uncertainty. Historically, business leaders, coaches, and military leaders don't tackle the issue of grief in the workplace well. And yet what they do about these has a huge financial and performance impact—for better or worse.

We have friends, colleagues, and teammates right now who are struggling through different phases of anxiety and stress while attempting to navigate their way through a global pandemic and unsteady economic circumstances. Some are facing a high operations tempo, others profound isolation.

Your response; your capacity to help your team navigate the uncertainty, the anxiety, the feelings of powerlessness; your capacity to help reduce the stigma around asking for help while still enabling your team to remain productive and focused on their Span of Control—that all comes down to your mindset.

A basic understanding of how our brains work is key to mastering mindset challenges.

A BASIC UNDERSTANDING OF HOW OUR BRAINS WORK IS KEY TO MASTERING MINDSET CHALLENGES.

Ever notice that the moment you crawl into bed after a long day, you find yourself dwelling on all the bad stuff? A coworker's criticisms are on playback far more than your kid's compliments, and fixating on your failures seems like the most natural stream of your consciousness. Even when you are aware of this habit, it can be hard to break—especially when it gathers force during your quietest moment of the day. The demons and negative self-talk have uncanny staying power.

Turns out there's a name for this dynamic.

Psychologists call it *negative bias*, and in a nutshell, it means that negative events have a greater impact on our brains than positive ones. As you might guess, negative bias can have a powerful effect on your life.

Psychologist John Cacioppo has conducted several studies where participants were shown pictures of positive, negative, or neutral images while their brain activity was observed. The results? Negative images produced a stronger response in the cerebral cortex than positive or neutral images. This surge in activity suggests that our behaviors and attitudes tend to be shaped more powerfully by bad news and experiences.

There are a few other reasons for our inclination to dwell on the negative.

Studies have shown that bad news is more likely to be perceived as truthful. Since negative information draws greater attention, it also may be seen as having greater validity. This might be why bad news seems to get more attention.[21]

And then there's the threat I'll call "the cynic in all of us." Everyone has heard of the glass-half-empty and glass-half-full comparison. Those who see a glass partially filled as partially *full* tend to have a more positive outlook, or a *gain* mentality, while those who see it as partially *empty* tend to have a more negative one, or a loss mentality.

When it comes to our mindsets, we tend to believe "that's just how I'm wired." But is it possible to switch our outlooks and mentalities? Can we move beyond a penchant for the negative? What power do we really have to stop "circling the drain"?

Flip the Script

There's research indicating just how difficult it is to switch mindsets.

In a study testing how easily people could convert from one mindset to another, researchers told participants, "Imagine there's been an outbreak of an unusual disease, and six hundred lives are at stake." One group was asked the question, "If a hundred lives are saved, how many will be lost?" Another group was asked, "If a hundred lives are lost, how many will be saved?"

In other words, every participant had to make the same calculation—six hundred minus a hundred equals five hundred—but whereas people in one group had to convert from gains to losses, people in the second group had to convert from losses to gains.

The researchers timed how long it took participants to solve this simple math problem and found that when people had to convert from gains to losses, they could solve the problem quite quickly; it took them about seven seconds on average. But when people had to convert from losses to gains, it took them far longer, almost eleven seconds. This suggests that once we think about something as a loss, that way of thinking about it tends to stick in our heads and resist our attempts to change it.[22]

Does the suggestion that we all have a fundamental tendency to tilt toward negativity mean we can't improve our capacity to tilt toward positivity?

Nope.

It means that we have to *work* to see the upside of things.

We have to fight for our happiness.

We have to strive for excellence and combat complacency.

We have to struggle to find the silver lining.

Because seeing things on the bright side isn't natural, we have

to practice positive thinking on a regular basis. Consider what that would look like for you personally or for your team or organization. The first thing that comes to mind for me is to **never let a well-done project, accomplishment, task, or job go by without at least acknowledging it as well done.**

Remember my claim from earlier: you set the tone.

For me, debriefing is one way to ensure that we pause to recognize a job well done while also acknowledging what's not working so that we can make positive improvements.

In the US Navy Blue Angel debriefs, after every flight, they discuss what worked, what didn't, and they break down every single maneuver. Debriefing can take twice as long as the flight, and the criticisms are specific, brutal, and all geared toward getting better for the next flight, getting closer to ensuring that the maneuvers both look good and are safe. As part of the debriefing process, each pilot admits to their mistakes and says at the end, "I made this mistake, and I can fix it. Glad to be here." The effect is that everyone knows that a mistake was made, knows that corrective action will be taken, and the whole process breeds trust and confidence in the team while ending on a positive note.

In standard Navy and Marine Corps debriefs, we actually write on our debrief boards "Goods/Others" columns. We always end with taking the time to acknowledge and point out what is working, to celebrate our success.

Just like you have to practice being grateful, you have to practice finding the positives. If you don't take the time to appreciate what's going well, you've lost an opportunity to build morale, cohesion, and esprit de corps.

Our tendency to pay more attention to the negative and overlook the positive is likely a result of evolution. Earlier in human history focusing on negative threats in the world was *literally* a matter of life and death. Those who were more aware of the danger around them were more likely to survive.

But we know that our ultimate aim in the modern world is to *thrive*, not just survive. Your daily commute does not typically involve escaping the clutches of a bear, and your dinner is hopefully not dependent on your ability to kill a deer in

> OUR ULTIMATE AIM IN THE MODERN WORLD IS TO *THRIVE*, NOT JUST SURVIVE.

the woods. This means that with less fear and more focus, you can shift your attention away from your negative bias and toward all the good stuff that fills your day.

And if you're not sure where you or your team stands when it comes to negative bias, you might look for signs like these:

- less collaboration

- more demand for information and transparency from leadership

- less productivity

- more safety issues

- lashing out at coworkers

- worse patient or client outcomes

- a high rate of turnover

- absent in action (they are showing up, but they are not really "there"; they're disengaged)

As you and your team struggle to absorb and understand all of the swirling uncertainty, there may also be more gossiping, complaining, and an inability to find solutions.

As a leader, your goals should be to:

- Communicate clearly and frequently so that your team has accurate information in times of uncertainty.

- Be predictable and consistent.

- Know your people well enough to get them the resources they need to manage crises.

- Reinforce your organization's values, and let your teammates know *why* they are valuable.

- Be calm. Your bearing matters.

- Ask them how they are doing and what you can do to help.

- Say "thank you" to let your teammates know they are valued.

- Acknowledge and celebrate success!

Too often I work with teams that move too quickly from one goal to the next, from one challenge to another without ever even taking the time to acknowledge the good work done.

During times of uncertainty and high-ops tempo, if you're not taking a second to say, "Thank you," to send the chocolates, or specifically call out and waggle a virtual high-five to your teammates across Zoom or Webex who are doing a great job? That's a lost opportunity to boost morale, to remind your team that the work they do matters, and to show that you value them.

Attaboys cost very little, but teammates who don't feel valued can cost you everything. The truth is, happiness, feeling valued, and achievement are tightly intertwined.

Encouragement and appreciation shouldn't be saved just for the end of a project or process. As fighter pilots, for example, we were constantly shifting between nonstop risk management and trying to maintain a positive, can-do attitude in challenging, life-or-death circumstances. That meant we needed encouragement and appreciation from the very start, even during the planning phase of our flights and missions.

We had a process called the Red Team that we used to identify flaws, inconsistencies, overlooked threats, and missed opportunities within a plan before we finalized that plan and moved on to the execution phase. The Red Team (a group unfamiliar with the plan) was called in to challenge us, to poke holes in what we came up with. Aside from exposing problem areas within our plan, the dialogue that we would have among team members would allow people to share best practices, different approaches, expertise, and knowledge across the team. Then we could take action to amend the plan as necessary. This further increased our chances for success *and* helped to create buy-in—a critical component to high performance.

Why does this matter?

The Red Team was a way of creating positive experiences and a sense of ownership and agency within our teams.

Our brains are literally designed to hang on to negative experiences and negativity like Velcro and to perceive these situations as threats to our survival. Red Teaming gave us a sense of control, a sense that we were making progress from the very start.

A POSITIVE ATTITUDE WON'T GUARANTEE YOUR SUCCESS, BUT A NEGATIVE ATTITUDE KILLS YOUR ABILITY TO ADAPT.

A positive attitude won't guarantee your success, but a negative attitude kills your ability to adapt.

It is incumbent upon you, regardless of your rank, position, or title, to help create an environment even in times of uncertainty that can help dissipate fear and anxiety and help manage your teammates' expectations.

EMBRACE THE SUCK

In the Navy, we say you should "embrace the suck." What does that mean? Just what it sounds like: recognize that hard, challenging work is a part of getting to your goal. Sometimes, some of what you have to do sucks, and you're going to have to do it anyway. Things won't always go as planned. Your commitment, your grit, your resiliency will be tested. It's during those times that we have to remain flexible and be willing to continue to put in the work.

Embracing the suck *isn't* a negative or fatalistic response. In fact, it actually requires a positive attitude. It's similar to the improv technique called "yes, and ... " where you take whatever line or situation your improv partner offers you and work with it to build toward a goal.

You don't have to like or approve of what sucks. Instead, you're recognizing that a situation or a task is what it is, and you're taking a more positive attitude toward it.

Right now take a look around. You may be surrounded with some sucky stuff. It could be the growing pile of laundry, the sink full of dirty dishes, the supply chain that is struggling, channel partners that are drowning in uncertainty, the employees who are demanding much more of your time. Whatever your eyes happen to land on, embrace it.

Intentionally notice the positives. You *have* clothes that can pile up. You *have* dishes to get dirty. You *have* a supply chain and channel partners to work with. You *have* a team that might be driving you mad right now that just needs a little TLC and maybe some more *attaboys*.

These mini positive-noticing practices can become transformational. Embrace the suck—keep a sense of humor, show warmth to your team, and leave your lines of communication open.

Positive Reappraisal

Imagine that you're stuck in traffic. Your GPS is busted, your phone is dead, and you have no idea how to get where you need to go. After mumbling a little "FML … " you need to ask yourself, "What is within my Span of Control right now?" You cannot change the traffic patterns or the fender bender up ahead that's causing the huge delay. You cannot fix the broken GPS, nor can you beat yourself up over the fact that you left your phone charger at home (again). For this situation, the strategy we turn to is "positive reappraisal."[23] In science-speak: "Positive reappraisal is a critical component of meaning-based coping that enables individuals to adapt successfully to stressful life events."[24]

In other words, positive reappraisal might mean recognizing that sitting in traffic—lost and alone—is worth it (time to listen to that podcast you've had queued for a few months now!). It means deciding that unanticipated problems (even the discomfort and frustration that comes with them) have *value* by reframing the difficulties as opportunities for growth and learning.[25]

There are certain hardships we all experience regularly, if not daily: Mistakes. Failure. Fear. Pain. Lack. Our internal monologue might run something like this: *I dropped the ball at work. Am I really qualified for this position? Ugh, this is all starting to take its toll. Am I going to get sick? I don't even want to work in this field—I always wanted to work in politics. I'm not even halfway through my emails, and it's six o'clock …*

By recommending positive reappraisal, please know I'm not suggesting that you happy-unicorn-butterfly-Holly-go-lightly bullshit the situation. This is about intentionally reframing what you're faced with so that you can remain effective.

Too often change, chaos, and uncertainty overwhelm us to the point of paralysis (a.k.a. the freeze response or autopilot setting) and keep us from moving toward the life, business, or team we want. We know now that we tend to focus and dwell on the negative, and that negativity bias has to do with where we direct our *attention*. By directing more of our attention toward positive things, we can begin to shift our mindset.

When we shift our attention toward the positive, we begin to understand that:

- Failure is wisdom.

- Fear is excitement.

- Pain is information.

- Effective planning matters.

- Goals can be targeted for impact.

- **Action conquers fear.**

That endless and negative inner monologue can become a bit brighter and a heck of a lot more productive and intentional.

You're not always going to feel positive right away, of course, but that's not what this technique is about. This is about shifting your point of view—understanding and acknowledging reality, being clear about where you are trying to go, developing a game plan, and communicating it clearly to your team (or yourself!).

You can cultivate a winning, can-do attitude regardless of whether you're having a great day or a frustrating one.

My good friend Bill McCarthy, executive vice president of Worldwide Field Operations at Infoblox, is famous for using the phrase "we got 'em right where we want 'em!" whenever something unexpected or awful happens. It may seem like a joke, but it's more than that because it has the effect of quickly turning attention to figuring out how to move things forward toward a desired goal.

Bill also shared with me the following: "As a leader, you do not have the privilege to wear your negative emotions on your sleeve." That means when you have a bad day, you don't get the luxury of dwelling on it or taking it out on your team. Find a way to remain positive by being forward-looking; think of obstacles as opportunities. Don't be fooled into thinking this is artificial optimism; this is part of the mindset of a fearless leader.

Modeling that positive spirit, maintaining your bearing, your composure, and focusing on what *is* within your Span of Control—all are traits and habits that high-performing leaders exhibit and use.

To recap: your mindset is the dividing line between thriving and merely surviving. It would be nice if you could simply snap your fingers and automatically become more positive, more confident, and more resilient, but *trust me*—these things don't happen overnight. Building your mindset takes time and training, but the benefit is that it allows you to be *ready for the good* as much as for the bad and the ugly.

YOUR MINDSET IS THE DIVIDING LINE BETWEEN THRIVING AND MERELY SURVIVING.

EIGHT TIPS TO BETTER FOCUS ON THE GOOD AND BOOST YOUR RESILIENCE

1. **Clarify your Span of Control.** Shocker, right? Don't waste your time and energy trying to change circumstances you can't control. Even if you can't change a stressful situation, you have a choice when it comes to how you respond. Accepting what you cannot change allows you to focus on the things you can control.

2. **Focus on what really matters.** Understand what really matters to you—your core values, your purpose. What are the most important parts of your life today? Family? Fitness? Finances? Faith? Work? Community? Self-development? The legacy you want to leave? Focus your time and attention on the one or two things that matter most. Having too many priorities leads to overwhelm and overload! As we say in fighter aviation: "If you lose sight, you lose the fight."

3. **Use action to conquer fear.** Fear, anger, and disappointment can paralyze us, especially after a severe setback. It's human nature to assign blame rather than generate solutions. But fear doesn't have to hold you back. Get rid of all of the I-can'ts, Yeah-buts, I-should-haves, and I'll-never-be-able-tos. Focus on solutions, not setbacks.

4. **Learn from your experiences.** Red Team during planning. Debrief regularly. You can use the power of questions to gain focus and learn valuable lessons. Look for the root cause of a problem and then brainstorm solutions. Ask:
   □ What happened?
   □ Why is it good that this happened?
   □ How can I turn this around?

5. **Be grateful.** I said it before, and I'll say it again! Tell your team "thank you." On a personal level, writing for a few minutes each

day about things that you're grateful for can dramatically boost your happiness and well-being and even your health. Check in with yourself, and remember to *tilt toward the good.*

6. **Get beyond the bad.** We know that bad things tend to stick with us, so just be aware of that. One insult can stick with somebody all day—all week, even—and bad feelings tend to propagate themselves, right? Somebody flips you off at a stoplight, and then you lay on your horn at another driver moments later. But what if the next time somebody snapped at you, you took control *of you*? We can train and reconstruct our mindsets if we put some effort into doing so.

7. **Share the good.** We tend to think that misery loves company, that venting will help get rid of our negative emotions, or that we'll feel better if we just talk about how terrible our day was. So we talk about the mean boss, the date who never called us back, and the pitch meeting that bombed. But we forget to talk about the good stuff. And yet that's exactly where our minds need the most practice. So focus on the good. Share the good. Spread the good.

FOCUS ON THE GOOD. SHARE THE GOOD. SPREAD THE GOOD.

8. **Set realistic (but optimistic) expectations.** Expectations are a point of contention. You might have heard the ol' adage "expectations are premeditated resentments," whereas others believe that having high expectations is the key to success. In either case, expecting life to always turn out the way you want is a surefire way to disappoint yourself, because, as Span of Control teaches us, not all things are within our control. The paradox of expectation is solvable. *The outcome we get is a matter of how we navigate the things we can and cannot control.* Having high expectations *of what we can control* is beneficial.

Staying rooted in reality is crucial for building a healthy mindset that's capable of overcoming even the toughest of times. I'll say it again for emphasis: positive reappraisal is *not* about being overly positive or seeing cotton-candy clouds when a tornado is coming. With positive reappraisal, you see the situation for what it is and acknowledge what's difficult, you maintain perspective, and you identify the part of that experience that is worth it or that presents an opportunity for a positive outcome.

Here's a great example from the Navy. Vice Admiral James Stockdale was one of the legendary heroes of the Vietnam War. After his A-4 Skyhawk was shot down just south of Hanoi in North Vietnam, and as one of the senior ranking officers in the prison camp known as the Hanoi Hilton, he endured and survived seven and a half years of torture, interrogation, and solitary confinement at the hands of the Communist Vietnamese.

Even though the situation and threats changed daily, staying rooted in reality—being clear about the real risks of death, what it would take to survive—and blending those with a bit of faith in that very survival, that's what kept him alive. This dualistic thinking, commonly known as the Stockdale Paradox, is summed up best by Stockdale himself: **"You must never confuse faith that you will prevail in the end—which you can never afford to lose—with the discipline to confront the most brutal facts of your current reality, whatever they might be."**

In Jim Collins's *Good to Great*, Stockdale had a conversation with Collins about how his approach was different from that of the camp's optimists. When asked who didn't make it out of the camp, Stockdale responded, "The optimists. Oh, they were the ones who said, 'We're going to be out by Christmas.' And Christmas would come, and Christmas would go. Then they'd say, 'We're going to be out by Easter.' And Easter would come, and Easter would go. And then Thanksgiving, and then it would be Christmas again. And they died of a broken heart."[26]

So often our natural inclination is to do anything and everything to avoid, internalize, or ignore the problems at hand (the good ol' shut down, compartmentalize, channelize, or indulge our coping mechanisms). Or we'll flip the autopilot switch and not do anything to better our current habits—even when it comes down to choices around our most fundamental activities.

But the key to positive reappraisal and choosing to fight for joy is to look the problems we're facing dead in the eyes, believing we will survive them. A positive mindset is about acknowledging reality and moving forward faster. It's about taking back control of our minds and not letting what is easier—that negative bias—take over.

It is always—and I mean *always*—within our Span of Control to change our mindset.

Mindset matters. Success is not just about a great strategy or tactics. It comes down to focusing on your Span of Control, staying predictable, and tending to your own and your teams' emotional needs.

A positive attitude or mindset doesn't guarantee success, but a negative one will kill your ability to adapt.

If you take positive, decisive actions, you can improve your capacity to withstand adversity, bounce back from setbacks, and not only survive but thrive. Your positive attitude toward change and the ability to be flexible and adaptable will determine your level of success and overall happiness.

We all want to conquer chaos, seize control, and achieve our wildest dreams. But no matter what any self-help guru tells you, those things are *never going to come just by positive visualization.* That's just baloney.

It's going to take hard work and constant brain training.

Mindset matters. Success is not just about a great strategy or tactics. It comes down to focusing on your Span of Control, staying predictable, and tending to your own and your teams' emotional needs.

—CAREY LOHRENZ

Don't shy away. Confront reality, no matter how brutal, and don't lose faith. Everything might just work out, and your dreams very well might come true. That, my friends, is the paradox.

THE FEEL FACTOR

How often do you say things like, "I am tired," "I am burned out," and "I am upset"?

Turns out when we use "I am" statements, the neurotransmitters in our brain are telling our body that we *are* indeed those negative thoughts.

Let's say you had a rough morning at the office. Nothing seemed to go right. Meetings got canceled, clients got snarky and sweat the small stuff, calls didn't go through. You got fed up and told yourself, "I am so annoyed with today; I am clearly not good enough for anyone around here." As the day went on, you started to really feel that way, and those feelings carried with you throughout your entire week.

By saying "I am annoyed" and "I'm not good enough," your brain works to communicate that to the rest of your body so that you'll start feeling *more* annoyed and doubt yourself more.

Next time you catch your self-talk resembling this pattern, take a good, hard look at your bad, hard day and try changing just a bit what you say about it: "I *feel* annoyed about today and the way it's going, and I wish people would notice all the hard work I'm doing."

Not only do these little shifts reframe your perspective, they will also change the way your body registers negativity.

In the next week, try to listen to the words you use. Tally how many times you say **am** when it's paired alongside a feeling. My bet is you might catch yourself more often than you think.

Facing Self-Doubt

If you think that neutrality or shying away from challenges beats negativity, let me tell you outright that the effects are quite the same.

The decision to lead, and lead well, is highly personal. I've seen many people back away from great leadership opportunities, spouting lines like "I'm not sure I'm ready" and "I just think it's too soon" and "I still have some growing to do." These statements, though masquerading as neutral, are actually negative. They almost always mask insecurity and a desire to avoid the challenges that come with leadership. These statements are the fear talking—and it's saying self-defeating things.

Nine times out of ten, fear is telling you a bullshit story.

Everyone has his or her own personal self-doubts and fears to face. It takes courage to lead. It takes courage to run an eight-figure P&L or start a business from scratch when everyone else around you is telling you not to do it.

I tell you this because these feelings are common to anyone who has accepted the challenge of leadership, the challenge of stepping into the breach, the challenge of going after big, audacious goals.

After years of coaching leaders and businesspeople, I've seen self-doubt plague those who face their first leadership role or a step up into a larger, more challenging role. Self-doubt can even stymie those who have been in a leadership role for years but who suddenly find themselves struggling to lead through uncertainty and chaos.

Maybe the skills that brought you success up to this point are no longer valid. (I'm not talking about core values of integrity and leading ethically; those should never change.) Or maybe the time spent on the things that you value must change as your responsibility level changes. Leaders who aren't able to shove that hesitancy to the side, identify what matters most, be bold in their convictions, and then take action won't do well.

Having the courage to take the first step on a new leadership journey, regardless of tenure, is never easy. But if you don't do it, you're bound to miss out on becoming the leader and person you could have been. If I hadn't had the courage to apply to Aviation Officer Candidate School—and then keep pushing until I was holding the stick of an F-14—I would've missed out on serving my country *and* flying the amazing airplane I was so passionate about.

You will run into turbulence. You will feel vulnerable at times. You will have to lean into the unknown. You will need to carry on when you'd rather quit. You will have to learn to navigate difficulties with humility, grace, and grit and to be undaunted by the future.

That said, quelling self-doubt requires that you don't look so far into the future that you become overwhelmed or paralyzed into inaction. Instead, try looking to the past for inspiration. For four thousand years, people have managed through "unprecedented" times. Remember that you are not the first person to embark on or face down something "new."

Nor am I. Remembering that gives me perspective on my own sense of purpose in the world.

My path to entrepreneurship was by no means easy. It didn't happen overnight, and it didn't follow some influencer's BS list of "Seven Steps to Business Owner Success." At times, it felt remarkably messy, and there have been significant learning experiences along the way.

But I'm dedicated to learning: from those who have gone before me, from my colleagues and mentors, and from the people I most want to help. If I hadn't worked on developing the confidence and the courage, the mindset and mental frameworks, and if I hadn't invested time in relationships and advisors, I might not have built up the belief that as long as I keep learning and keep taking action—*I'll figure it out.* I would never have been able to build a business that has impacted and elevated millions of other people, helping *them* to harness their potential, make better decisions, build stronger teams, and focus on what matters most.

To me, that would have been too high a price to pay for the comfort of saying "I'm not sure I'm ready."

FOCUS QUESTIONS

- What have you learned about yourself from times of adversity?

- When, or regarding what, do you most doubt yourself?

- When was the last time you expressed gratitude or shared something good? How did that feel?

Chapter 6

GROW YOUR GROWTH MINDSET

've gone through a lot of transitions in my life. I call it going from Mach 2 to preschool and back again.

I've had jobs mucking stalls, riding show horses, turning corn, drying doorjambs at a carwash, bartending, working retail, working for a nonprofit, being a fighter pilot, being a mom, being an entrepreneur, running a seven-figure business. I've been sued by someone trying to silence my voice. I've stood on stages in front of twenty-eight thousand people, coached Olympic and professional athletes, been an association president and a board member …

Were there times that I took a leap of faith leveling up, going for it before I "felt ready"? Absolutely.

Were there times that I waited and studied and prepped and maintained an unrelenting work pace and rhythm, or stayed in a job or position too long because I was trying to get as close to mastery as possible, as close to derisking the situation as possible? Absolutely.

But regardless of the uncertainty, regardless of the outcome in any of those scenarios, somewhere deep down I knew, and still know, that whatever happens, I'll figure it out.

Part of that may be personality, part of that may be upbringing, but part of that is the by-product of practice, of taking chances again and again, and of being committed to learning.

My mom's side of the family hails from the Deep South. She was one of ten children and grew up dirt poor and surrounded by love. All of the kids were expected to work at a very young age; picking cotton in the fields, shelling pecans in the groves, babysitting neighbors' kids—anything to help the family survive. They were also expected to be of service—to the church, their communities, their neighbors.

You know already that my dad's parents were Hungarian and Dutch immigrant families. Two different languages, two different religions, one huge commonality: an unbreakable work ethic and belief that how you show up matters. Doing good work, keeping the faith, and contributing to something other than yourself was honorable, admirable, and expected.

Both my grandparents were voracious readers and were constantly learning new things: taxidermy, crochet, world history. My grandpa went from being a professional boxer to working the assembly lines at the AMC car factory. Yes, at one time, they had a Pacer. My grandma stood on the factory floor for over forty years working at Western Publishing, helping bind, box, and sort millions of Little Golden Book books. Chances are if you've ever read *The Poky Little Puppy* or *Scuffy the Tugboat*, my grandma may have had a hand on your book.

My mom ended up being a flight attendant before being forced to give that up because she got married (as went the regulations in the 1960s—that's what women were forced to do by company policy, yikes), and my dad was a former USMC aviator, who then flew as a test pilot and after that for a major airline.

From all of them, my brother and I learned that on the road to any worthwhile accomplishment or achievement, you're going to hit obstacles and barriers to success. We learned that no matter how gifted, talented, passionate, blessed, hopeful, hardworking, or creative you may be—*you are entitled to nothing.* And we learned that without the willingness to keep at something, success in any way, shape, or form simply will not be possible.

> NO MATTER HOW GIFTED, TALENTED, PASSIONATE, BLESSED, HOPEFUL, HARD-WORKING, OR CREATIVE YOU MAY BE—*YOU ARE ENTITLED TO NOTHING.*

That means I'm someone who trusts in the process, the habit of doing the work, the habit of investing in reading—a lot. I'm someone who sees that even when the outcome isn't what I want it to be, I'll have learned something. A valuable lesson. A nugget to take me into the next chapter. A bit of wisdom to carry and pay forward. I'm someone who invests in training, in education, and I've learned to ask for help, feedback, and guidance from those I respect, those who have already proven to be successful and who operate with integrity.

I think that too often people are looking for the instant life hack, the quick fix, the fail-safe way to live and be successful, and they want certainty in the outcome. For these reasons, they'll play it safe when it comes to taking chances—or risks—that might bring them joy.

But playing it safe, playing it small? That's no way to make an impact. There will be rejection. There will be disappointments. There may be big losses. Because if you're not failing, you're probably not pushing yourself hard enough.

Read that again: if you are not failing, you're not pushing yourself hard enough. Yes, *even in times of crisis*. Although you may have to throttle back on your number's goals, the foundational idea of focusing on what you can control and not getting sucked into that which you can't? That still has to be your mantra.

That mantra works against complacency, and it works against fear, because it emphasizes that the *only* way to move forward is by taking action.

Action conquers fear.

Pushing yourself or your team may look different now than it did nine, twelve, or eighteen months ago. But the turbulence we are currently facing favors those who can nimbly adapt and adjust, not just go head down like a bull in a china shop.

Even in times of crisis, we should be focused on developing new or shifted practices while we also stay mindful of our best practices. It's precisely times of uncertainty in which we can't be afraid to have courageous conversations, to address the fear and vulnerability that we and our teams might feel when the path ahead is unclear. You may need to address legacy issues, products, habits, and practices that are tough to let go of.

Crisis, in any industry, demands *more* from us as leaders, owners, board members, heads of households. We have to be willing to ask *more* questions of our team and our partners than ever before, questions like:

- What options do you see?

- What am I missing?

- What's my/our blind spot?

- What do you suggest?

We can't simply hunker down and wait for the storm to pass. And we must acknowledge that adapting and adjusting successfully in times of crisis is a process, a marathon run that requires resilience on our parts.

A mindset of knowing that without great risk there *cannot* be great reward is a growth mindset. Learning and failing, and learning and failing again is the cost of that reward.

Shifting from Fixed to Growth

After decades of research, world-renowned Stanford University psychologist Carol S. Dweck discovered a simple but groundbreaking truth—at the end of the day, there are essentially two mindsets: the fixed mindset and the growth mindset. These mindsets determine how a person judges his or her own abilities, talents, potential, and intelligence. If you have a fixed mindset, you believe that your qualities are unchangeable, that you are stuck with whatever intelligence, creative abilities, or personality traits you have now. With a fixed mindset, you tend to fear challenges because you see potential failure as a threat.

For fixed-mindset people, setbacks are catastrophic. After all, if who you are is so tightly linked with a small category of things you are good at, then failure at anything else attacks your very core. With that mindset, failing at something means *you* are a failure. These individuals hold the belief that trying and failing is worse than not trying at all.

People with a growth mindset, on the other hand, believe that they can develop and strengthen their basic qualities through effort and constant learning. This mindset recognizes that yes, people are different, but everyone can improve and grow their talents, abilities, and even intelligence *through effort and experience.*[27]

Smart people succeed, says the fixed mindset. If you succeed, you're a smart person, and if you don't succeed, you must not be smart.

People can get smarter, says the growth mindset. If you pick the hard problem, you like the challenge of stretching yourself. Failure is simply a means of learning something that will help you succeed another time.

People can get smarter, says the growth mindset. If you pick the hard problem, you like the challenge of stretching yourself. Failure is simply a means of learning something that will help you succeed another time.

—CAREY LOHRENZ

Understanding your mindset and how it drives your *potential* is critical. Some of us can have both a fixed and growth mindset, depending on the task or situation we're facing. Hang with me on this one. I know I think of myself as being mostly a growth-mindset type of person. But I can get beaten down. When I hear enough times from those people who want to see me fail, who say I'm not good enough, smart enough, invested enough—whatever that "enough" value is that they ascribe to me—and when their assault is nonstop? It can wear on me, exhaust me. It can cause me to doubt my capabilities and second-, third-, and fourth-guess myself.

But I also know from experience that it's hard being a pioneer. It's challenging to be under a white-hot spotlight.

You will make mistakes.

You will get kicked in the teeth.

It can be brutal.

Go anyway.

Take action.

In *Fearless Leadership*, I shared what it takes to step up in spite of challenges in order to stop flying under the radar.

Especially for leaders who are women or BIPOC, if you want to fulfill your potential or develop the most capable team—regardless of your gender, race, or industry—you must understand that *people will react against any assumptions or "norms" you appear to shatter.*

For example, research has shown us that in order to conform, women need to be willing to play a small game and avoid rocking the boat. We're expected not to assert ourselves, not to carry around an extra ten pounds, and certainly not to let people know that we are kicking ass in our jobs.

But playing small serves *nobody*.

The pressures to conform to expectations present a daily struggle for those women I know (and even some men) who are currently climbing the ladder—and even for those who have made it to the top. Playing small, trying to blend in, making nice, flying under the radar—these norms, unfortunately, are not obsolete or irrelevant.

Stop flying under the radar. Knowing your value, speaking up, staying tenacious, and *not* flying under the radar will be required to continue to grow.

As my dad used to say, "Those who tell you 'you can't' and 'you won't' are probably the ones most scared you will."

If you want to change your orientation to a growth or learning mindset, know that's exactly where Span of Control comes into play.

The overwhelming majority of high performers—executives, military leaders, athletes, business owners, health care workers, first responders, and entrepreneurs—have a growth mindset. We all know that when the pressure is on, we do *not* focus on factors outside of our control, and we continue to do the hard work of focusing on learning and improving.

We can change our mindset by choosing to make that change. We actually *get to choose* how we think about setbacks. Instead of automatically throwing up our hands at the first signs of defeat or resistance, or blaming others for the current situation we find ourselves in, or doomscrolling social media nonstop because it feels easier than taking action—we can decide to make the effort to determine our success.

WE CAN DECIDE EXACTLY HOW WE WILL FRAME OUR CHALLENGES.

We can decide exactly how we will frame our challenges.

It doesn't mean it's easy, far from it. But it *is* a choice we all can make.

And you've survived your worst days so far, right? Which means you've got a chance—even if you're feeling like you're currently at ground zero or drowning.

You've got a chance.

How? Focus on what is within your Span of Control.

- **Stop obsessing over the bad stuff.** That's not useful. Stuff happens. If you can't control it? Learn from it and move on. Find the opportunities.

- **Tilt toward the good.** Name three things right now that are good. In our family, every night at dinner we go around the table and do "Good Day, Bad Day." We list the bad things that happened, but we always have to follow it up with three good things. Sounds corny, I know. **But it works.** It's *practicing* positive reappraisal.

- **Identify what's working and what's not.** What is the most useful thing you could do right now? Solve what you can, and continue moving forward. momentum develops and healing comes when you keep moving forward.

PTSD vs. PTG

You've likely heard of posttraumatic stress disorder—PTSD. It affects almost eight million US adults and can occur at almost any age, including in children. PTSD sufferers may be victims of physical, emotional, or sexual assault; accidents; natural disasters; military combat; or overwhelming, continuous stress that causes hopelessness. Not everyone who has PTSD has physically been through a traumatic event; some people experience symptoms when a loved one goes through something traumatic. PTSD symptoms can include having intrusive memories of the traumatic event, avoidant behavior, negative thinking and mood, and changes in physical and emotional reactions, like being easily startled by the slightest of things. There can also be secondary stressors that add to the original trauma, sometimes leading to depression, anxiety, withdrawal from normal activity, insomnia, and substance abuse.

But what about posttraumatic *growth*? Yes, PTG. It's a real term, a real condition, but my guess is that you're unfamiliar with it. Over the last ten years, I've asked thousands of people in my audiences whether they've heard of PTG. Only one hand has gone up. Clearly, we are missing out on one of the key elements of a growth mindset.

Research shows that only a very small percentage of people actually suffer long-term effects of PTSD after a traumatic event. (To be clear, PTSD is different from traumatic brain injury, which poses its own challenges.) Richard G. Tedeschi and Lawrence Calhoun coined the term posttraumatic growth in 1995 at the Posttraumatic Growth Research Group at the University of North Carolina. According to them, people who go through trauma and undergo posttraumatic growth flourish in life with a greater appreciation and greater resilience.[28] They define PTG as a "positive psychological change in the wake of struggling with highly challenging life circumstances."[29]

In other words, people who experience PTG are engaging in something like big-picture positive reappraisal.

Given the right support, the majority of us are able to put traumatic events into context and actually come through them stronger—with an improved sense of self, better relationships, recognition of new opportunities, and a greater appreciation for life.

As you might imagine, in order to maintain an effective and safe fighting force in the US military, we have to continuously work to maintain healthy (both mentally and physically) fit service members. That's not always an easy task considering the age demographic and wicked ops tempo.

But by having the conversation that a negative outcome or PTSD is not a foregone conclusion—combined with assessments evaluating the emotional, social, family, and spiritual fitness of each soldier, and then developing resilience training protocols—the military is able to enable a much more positive outcome for soldiers in stressful situations than for those who didn't receive any of those programs or training support.

There are at least two important elements of recovering from trauma.

- First, individuals have to find the capacity to do the personal work, to hold themselves accountable in order to find a path forward.

- Second, having the right supports in place—both people and systems—is a necessary part of moving forward productively.

- A third thing that helps? An intact sense of humor.

One of the unique characteristics of many high-performing military teams, be they fighter squadrons, special ops units, or Marine recon units, is the prevalence of gallows humor. It's not only a way to deflect distress in stressful, life-or-death situations but also a way to effectively manage stress.

Hỏa Lò Prison was originally a prison used by French colonists in French Indochina for political prisoners. It was later used by the North Vietnamese to house US prisoners of war and was one of the most brutal POW camps during the Vietnam War. An amazing story of that experience comes from USMC aviator Captain Orson Swindle. Capt. Swindle endured over seven years as a POW. While captive at the "Hanoi Hilton" (the same place where Vice Admiral Stockdale was held) and during one particularly brutal ten-day interrogation, Capt. Swindle's captors claimed the US had no culturally relevant holidays. He was able to convince them that indeed it did: a "National

Doughnut Day" celebrated on November 10. A few months later, on November 10, all of the POWs in the Hanoi Hilton were served up a few little doughnutlike treats.

What Capt. Swindle and the other POWs knew and their captors did not was that November 10 was the United States Marine Corps' birthday.

FINDING HUMOR IN THE DARKEST TIMES CAN BE A LIFELINE. IT NOT ONLY RELEASES STRESS, IT ALSO CAN BRIDGE ISOLATION, INSPIRE CREATIVITY, EVEN BREAK CRUSHING BOREDOM.

Finding humor in the darkest times can be a lifeline. It not only releases stress, it also can bridge isolation, inspire creativity, even break crushing boredom.

And it helps you maintain perspective.

Whenever one of my teammates or I were about to share a scary or bad flight story, we would always begin with the line "There I was, five hundred knots, out of gas and out of ideas." It would always be met with hoots and howls or an "Oh boy," and that's because joking about what was to come was also a way to acknowledge that we'd survived something sketchy, dangerous, and we were trying to embrace it. That bit of optimistic spin at the start was a way of letting everyone else know: no matter what, you can survive too.

Recovery from adversity and bouncing back to become even stronger takes time and patience, but it can happen for the majority of people. Challenges, when met with the right attitude, can become catalysts for growth.

Let's go back to Vice Admiral James Stockdale—who spent four of his eight years in the Hanoi Hilton in solitary confinement, two of those four years in heavy leg irons.

Here's a telling comment from him about the event of having his aircraft shot down: "On September 9, 1965, I flew at five hundred knots right into a flak trap, at treetop level, in a little A-4 airplane that I suddenly couldn't steer because it was on fire, its control system shot out. After ejection, I had about thirty seconds to make my last statement in freedom before I landed in the main street of a little village right ahead. And, so help me, I whispered to myself: 'Five years down there, at least.'"[30]

Your mindset, the one thing that is always within your Span of Control, will determine what is possible for you, your team, your organization, your family.

In all the executive programs I've conducted, the board meetings I've attended, the professional coaches and athletes I've worked with, and the incentive meetings I've been a part of, the common threads I find in everyone is that they are genuinely grateful for their opportunities, they are able to set their egos aside and show a common respect for each other, and they are remarkably upbeat and forward-looking. They are *intentionally* optimistic.

Hard times and uncertainty can stir up fear in most of us. But the ability to adapt under pressure, to stay solutions-oriented, will always serve you well.

Those top performers *expect* that bad things will happen. They harness the power of focusing on what is within their Span of Control and don't allow external factors to permanently throw them off course.

Difficulties and misfortune oftentimes define your strengths and weaknesses for you, whether you like it or not. You just have to be able to apply the lessons learned. The awareness gained from overcoming adversity—especially during those crucible moments—plays a significant role in determining your path to success. What you think of now as a big disappointment or huge stumbling block can become the launchpad to something greater.

Most people underestimate their ability to recover from trauma. As we have more in-depth conversations around PTSD, it's worth pointing out the potential for PTG. Bad things can have good side effects. Lessons can be learned, and people can be transformed. We *can* grow stronger, more positive, more resilient.

As Elie Wiesel, Holocaust survivor, Nobel laureate, author, and human activist once said, "There are victories of the soul and spirit. Sometimes, even if you lose, you win." With some effort, you can find the positive way forward, both every day and when facing adversity. You can take a lot more than you think you can, and you can love your life a lot more than you currently do.

FOCUS QUESTIONS

Think about a recent negative situation and ask yourself the following:

- Were there, or will there be, any positive outcomes that result from this situation?

- Did you learn anything from the situation?

- How did you (or might you) grow and develop as a result of this situation?

Chapter 7

MAKE GOOD DECISIONS

E arly on in my flying career, an instructor gave me some good advice: "Plan so that you know when to knock it off." "Knock it off" is a term we used when we got caught up in an unsustainable furball (a dogfight) or when we hit the hard deck (the agreed-upon altitude where we would no longer fight).

The instructor's point was this: make a plan, or at least think about and consider when—not *if*, but *when* you get engaged in a fight (or flight) that is either dangerous or unsustainable—you'll know to call a time-out or leave.

In the corporate world, we can think of it as having a well-thought-out exit strategy.

A monumental decision nearly everyone makes as some point, whether they're a leader, owner, entrepreneur or even partner (business or personal) is: Should I stay/continue or should I go/exit?

On more than one occasion, I've had to make a decision quickly that in the short-term would be difficult but in the long term would be critical for my businesses, my survival, and my sanity. And if you're in business, in a leadership position, or have owned your own business for any length of time, you've probably had to do this too. Maybe it's dropping a vendor who is no longer meeting expectations. Maybe it's ending a business partnership with a friend because one party isn't operating from the same set of values.

Regardless of the situation, your best chance of survival, your best chance of making a good decision under stress, is to be prepared—to think about your go/no-go criteria and your exit strategy *before* you have your back up against the proverbial wall. This way, when you hit that limiting factor, that previously identified exit point? You'll know it's time to bail, to knock it off.

With forethought, consideration, and planning, the ability to make good decisions gets easier over time. It's kind of like compounding interest: if you can learn from those stay-or-go situations, the impact on your future decisions can be lasting and positive.

Overthinking and Underperforming

When it comes to self-development, it's easy to give too much credit to the thinking mind. The mind is "right," *right?* Well, not necessarily.

The fastest route to getting overwhelmed is *over*thinking. We all fall into the vicious cycle of overthinking, which is why it's important

THE FASTEST ROUTE TO GETTING OVERWHELMED IS OVERTHINKING.

to remember that overthinking is fear's best friend. Both lead to bouts of stasis, and both keep us trapped in the makings of our own minds, deterred from pursuing the things we want most.

If you've heard me give a presentation, you've probably heard me share the phrase "Eighty percent is good enough!" ("Unless," I add, "you're one of the compliance or finance folks in the audience!") What I mean by that is that if you've taken the time beforehand to think through possible scenarios—the potential threats and obstacles—your chances of responding successfully to change are greatly improved, even if your plan isn't perfect, which it will *never* be. You have to learn to execute with a "good enough" plan—in aviation, we called this the "eighty percent solution."

You will not always have 100 percent of the information you need. Things change. Time keeps marching on. Partners crash. Vendors fail. Pandemics hit. We need to be able to take the next step, to take action. To avoid being at the mercy of an environment that is outpacing your plan, start executing your "good enough" plan sooner rather than later, and then plan to debrief afterward to capture lessons learned.

Delaying action while overanalyzing information doesn't help when it comes to getting things done. Overthinking and underperforming can be paralysis inducing.

So many of us sit around *thinking* about how we want to do something rather than actually *doing* it (sometimes we're even thinking about thinking about something). Instead of *absorbing* information, *adapting* to that information, and *acting* on that information, we fall prey to a tendency—at best—to absorb, ruminate, get overwhelmed, worry, and then ... stop.

Replaying yesterday's conversations in your head and dwelling on catastrophic outcomes aren't helpful. But solving a problem is. So ask yourself: Are you thinking or overthinking? Are you being proactive or just getting distracted? Are you searching for a solution or wallowing in self-pity? How many times have you analyzed whether or not you should make that phone call? How many times have you repeated the same concern to a colleague or friend without doing something about it?

If you're overthinking, change the channel in your brain. Acknowledge that your thoughts aren't helpful, and get involved in an activity that will get your brain focused on something more action-oriented.

Developing a bias to act—motion over emotion—was drilled into us at an early stage in AOCS. We had to refine and train our brains' abilities to cope with chaos and overwhelm.

I encourage you to get started changing the channel and seeing what happens. Right now that could be simply getting outside and moving your body, taking a walk around your house or apartment, doing a handful of pushups or sit-ups—anything to change your physical state. Then, after you've done that, sit back down at your computer, close all those open tabs in your browser, turn off notifications, and get to work.

That stuck feeling—the junction of fear, perfectionism, and distraction that stops us from moving forward—is only escapable if we make decisions to get unstuck. The cycle of fear and rationalization can end only if you take decisive *action*.

Successfully navigating fear comes down to having go-to action steps. You've got to find your seamless course of action within your Span of Control.

Does the quarterback have to think hard about what his next move is once he catches the ball?

Of course not.

When Navy fighter pilots need to land the plane, do you think they have to go pull out the aircraft manual to remember how to make a smooth landing?

Nope. Years of training make it almost automated.

Even when the circumstances are different—more chaotic, stressful, and uncertain—the responses and action steps are the same. *Meatball, line up, angle of attack.*

Making good decisions during times of chaos ultimately comes down to having good habits in place to quell anxiety.

Every decision we make essentially commits us to a course of action, and anyone who's practiced making lots of decisions in a particular field or at a specific job will tell you that their habits and routine behaviors are so ingrained that they don't need to give them much thought. Relying on those habits has become the *key* to their success.

The beauty of habits, after all, is that you don't have to *think* about them. They don't consume or control your every conscious thought. And the only way they become second nature is by consistent action. The key

THE KEY TO OVERCOMING CHAOS AND ACHIEVING LASTING SUCCESS IS CONSISTENT ACTION.

to overcoming chaos and achieving lasting success is consistent action. Our actions become our habits. Those habits become our capacity for "quick thinking" in situations that define our futures.

In chapter 2, we learned that our brains make nearly 35,000 decisions a day, and so the brain will kick into an automatic decision-making mode to protect itself—to save mental energy and free up consciousness to work on particularly demanding or important things. Here, we're learning about how our brains do this even when it comes to those most stressful circumstances.

We can influence those actions by training our brains in the use of mental models.

Meatball, line up, angle of attack.

Mental models shape how we understand the world—the connections we see, our understanding of how something works. These models are useful insofar as they help us to simplify what's complex into manageable chunks. Developing mental models requires training yourself in a series of habits, steps, or questions for how to think in an emergency so that you can respond almost effortlessly, remain focused on what matters, and ignore distractions. **Creating mental models (or patterns, concepts, and frameworks) helps you quickly understand, interpret, and assess a situation, and make better and better decisions about what to do next.** In other words? When you use a mental model, you are telling yourself a story or providing a script for what's happening as it's happening. These stories are how our brains decide what to pay attention to and what to ignore.

Habits and mental models have nothing to do with skill, financial position, education, or appearance. Anyone can learn to create a new habit. The right habits are the only things that separate you from the life you want to live. Tomorrow's great performance is today's great habit. That's good reason to work each day to get just a little bit better.

TOMORROW'S GREAT PERFORMANCE IS TODAY'S GREAT HABIT.

I know for me at the beginning of the COVID-19 global pandemic, my daily routines of traveling to events around the world, holding conference calls on the go, coaching executives at scheduled times—all those routines were shattered.

Quite suddenly, I was working from home full time, with four kids going to school virtually full time from home. I had to be hyper-responsive to the never-ending changes going on with my work—calls moving, inbox flooded with client crises, Zoom meetings that were hours long. Add in kids popping in and out and me cooking nonstop, and you can see how over a period of time, my planning habits fell by the wayside. Every darn day the apple cart was flipped over. Rescheduled calls and meetings became the norm, and everything I did felt so … *reactive*.

Fortunately, I got back on track by simplifying and going back to what had worked in the past: writing in fat Sharpie marker on a

Post-it Note my top three things to focus on.

That's it.

Post-it Note stuck to my computer.

With those three clearly stated goals as my guideposts, I could stay organized and on track.

How can you do the same? I'd suggest starting with a personal plan, one that includes both preparing and debriefing.

At the beginning of the day, before firing up any electronic device, grab a notebook, a planner, or your Post-it Notes, and start writing down your top three most important things to do. Then, at the end of the day, crosscheck what you did with what you intended to do. Write down what's working, what's not, and why. Debriefing *in writing* allows you to identify any shortfalls or gaps in performance and execution and can improve your ability to anticipate what your next best move should be.

Don't leave success to chance. Keep learning and staying focused on continuous improvement. Work toward getting just 1 percent better every day.

Catch, Locate, Throw

Imagine you are on the football field with pigskin in hand. A bunch of massive grown men are running toward you with the sole goal of taking that football away from you and your team by forcing you to the ground. Meanwhile there are thousands of screaming fans watching your every move. Talk about a moment of potential overwhelm!

In the time frame of a few chaotic seconds—before a linebacker crushes him into the turf—a quarterback has to make a series of quick, difficult choices. As the protective wall formed by his teammates begins to collapse, he must remain incredibly focused and in control, looking for some meaningful signal downfield amid the chaos.

People often think that the arm of the quarterback is what's important, that his ability to throw the ball accurately is the most valuable thing. But throwing the ball is the easy part—well, easy-ish. It's talent, strength, coaching, mechanics, and relentless intentional repetition and practice that help with throwing accuracy. But it's the decision-making process in the throes of game play that's the truly tricky part.

Think about it. We are used to watching football on television, getting a nice all-encompassing, bird's-eye view of the grassy stage. It looks easy, almost choreographed. Neat little Xs and Os doing their jobs.

However, as we know, football isn't ballet. It's a freaking battle. How on earth does a quarterback—ground-level, without that almost-omnipotent perspective—know how to make a good decision about where to throw the ball?

How does he absorb the chaos, act amid the chaos, and adapt to the chaos?

Even while he's surrounded by disorder, the quarterback has to stand relatively still and *focus*. He needs to look through and past the mayhem and make sense of all the moving pieces in light of what he knows he needs to do and what he needs to look out for.

Lots of time, energy, and money has gone into figuring the *why* and the *how* behind the quarterback's ability to make good choices—the NFL attempts time and time again to determine some kind of test or formula that can help separate the wheat from the chaff. In fact, the NFL requires all players to take what's called a Wonderlic intelligence test, which is essentially a mini-IQ test. The test is twelve minutes long and consists of fifty questions that get harder and harder as the test-taker proceeds.

Here's an example of an easy Wonderlic question: *Chain sells for*

$1.50 per foot. How many feet of chain can you buy for $18?[31]

The NFL assumes that players who are better at math and logic problems will make better decisions. Seems like a fair enough assumption, right? But time and time again, incredible quarterbacks score low, and the Wonderlic thesis proves, *eh*, not so wonderful. Turns out there is no real correlation between the results of the Wonderlic and the success of quarterbacks in the NFL.

So how do quarterbacks do it? What is the secret sauce to making a split-second *good* decision?

It's knowing that their one job—the single goal at that exact moment in time—is to catch that dang ball, locate the right teammate, and throw that ball to them. It's **keeping focused despite fear**. It's *meatball, line up, angle of attack* for quarterbacks. *Catch, locate, throw.*

It's being clear about what's within their Span of Control, and eliminating the distractions.

When it's game time and those quarterbacks are on the field, do you think they are worried about their broken dishwasher at home? Or the fight with a family member the night before? Or even if their contract will get reupped for the next season? Sure, minutes after the game, in the locker room, they may be stressing about all the other issues going on, but they know that in order to perform highly, they must concentrate on one thing and one thing only—the only thing that is within their control in that moment: to get the ball to the right teammate.

This unique ability to act amid chaos, to feel calm amid overwhelm, and to constantly be aware of their Span of Control— these are the skills that help quarterbacks get paid the big bucks. Each pass is really a guess, a speculation hurled through the air, but the best quarterbacks find ways to make *better* guesses.

Not perfect. But *better.*

When faced with pressure, you've got to replace perfect with *better* and fear with *focus*.

It's not about textbook trigonometry, perfect physics, or flawless logic. Imagine if a quarterback caught the ball and then suddenly started thinking about each and every possible option and outcome. *Face, meet turf. Ball, meet opponent.* Decision-making in that moment is about control, resilience, and action. There is no time to think; there is only time for a seamless chain of actions. That's Span of Control at work!

Fighter pilots aren't born with the ability to prioritize tasks in a high-pressure, high-stress environment; we learn the skills necessary to do so. We prepare relentlessly through hours spent studying, planning, briefing, debriefing, hours in simulators and ultimately in flight.

The same applies to quarterbacks. To make decisions amid the chaos and threats to their own physical well-being, they prepare relentlessly: they study, they plan, they brief, they debrief, and then they play. Not everyone wants to do that. It's hard. It takes time. It takes vulnerability to recognize your shortcomings. It takes patience. And grit. And tenacity. And asking for help.

Developing the capacity to make excellent decisions begins with understanding that you must take the time to learn, to fill in your knowledge gaps, to consider opposing views, to evaluate how what you're doing is wrong or not working well enough, as well as how it's right. That's how you deal with the unpredictable nature of a competitive, fast-moving, uncertain environment. All those things go into making intentional, specific, and thoughtful decisions.

When faced with pressure, you've got to replace perfect with *better* and fear with *focus.*

—CAREY LOHRENZ

ERADICATING PROBLEMS

Much of the time, we have too many problems taking up space in our heads, which leads to burnout, overwhelm, and sometimes a total breakdown. Being aware of what problems you can take off the table can help refine and sustain your focus.

Write down five current problems/issues in your life, and then decide which of them is within your Span of Control. If you realize that one of your problems is, say, what your mother-in-law thinks about you, go ahead and get a big ol' Sharpie and mark that one out. For those that are within your control, think of one action you can take today that could help you resolve just one aspect of that issue.

The Problem: _____

Is it within your control? ☐ Yes ☐ No

What action can you take?_____

The Problem: _____

Is it within your control? ☐ Yes ☐ No

What action can you take?_____

The Problem: _____

Is it within your control? ☐ Yes ☐ No

What action can you take?_____

The Problem: _____

Is it within your control? ☐ Yes ☐ No

What action can you take?_____

The Problem: _____

Is it within your control? ☐ Yes ☐ No

What action can you take?_____

A Bias for Action

All action is not equal—there is rash, and there is rational. There is lazy, and there is skilled. The key to better action is being intentional.

Be intentional in your choices, decisions, and actions.

In his book *The Obstacle Is the Way,* Ryan Holiday puts the point this way:

> **BE INTENTIONAL IN YOUR CHOICES, DECISIONS, AND ACTIONS.**

> What is action? Action is commonplace, *right* action is not. As a discipline, it's not any kind of action that will do, but *directed* action. Everything must be done in the service of the whole. Step by step, action by action, we'll dismantle the obstacles in front of us. With persistence and flexibility, we'll act in the best interest of our goals. Action requires courage, not brashness—creative application and not brute force. Our movements and decisions define us: We must be sure to act with deliberation, boldness, and persistence. Those are the attributes of right and effective action.

Nothing else—not thinking or evasion or aid from others. Action is the solution and the cure to our predicaments.[32]

Fighter pilots have to make multiple decisions in a fast-moving, dynamic environment with potentially dire or catastrophic consequences. We can't slow down or pull over to the side to deliberate.

Instead, we need to balance whatever tendency we have to risk-manage or to overthink with healthy doses of planning and constant learning. We've got to stop thinking that perfection is the only goal of taking action and learn to accept unavoidable failures. All of the talent in the world won't matter, whether you're a fighter pilot, a leader, or a financial planner, if you can't execute or avoid analysis paralysis or learn from your results.

WE NEED TO BALANCE WHATEVER TENDENCY WE HAVE TO RISK-MANAGE OR TO OVERTHINK WITH HEALTHY DOSES OF PLANNING AND CONSTANT LEARNING.

Sitting down and actually writing down a plan is *right* action—even if that plan is not perfect. Improving your ability to recognize when you're productively refining your plan or uselessly rehashing it again and again and again is critical to your success.

In AOCS, everything was done to weed out people who, when scared and under stress, didn't take the initiative and couldn't execute. Those people truly didn't understand, or didn't understand fast enough, how to develop what was called "a bias for action."

When you're trying to come aboard a pitching ship in a strike fighter aircraft at 165 miles per hour, or you're getting launched by a catapult—going from zero to more than 180 miles per hour in less than two seconds—and the air boss screams through the radio, "Tomcat off the bow! Eject! Eject! Eject!" *There is no gray area*. You don't ask questions or pause to think it over; you have to take action, or you will die.

That's why our instructors worked hard to establish a bias for action, passing only those student aviators who demonstrated that they would be instantly ready—thoroughly ready—to take on any challenge. What's drilled into all aspiring aviation officer candidates: Be flexible. Act decisively. Take the initiative. Don't wait to be told what to do. Your life and the lives of others depend on your ability to move forward and act.

Action conquers fear.

There's research to support that claim. Seymour Epstein of the University of Massachusetts at Amherst conducted a study in which novice parachute jumpers were fitted with heart-rate monitors that measured their pulse as the plane climbed upward toward its release point. He found that the jumpers' heart rates got faster and faster until just before they jumped. Once they were out of the plane, their heart rates declined dramatically.[33] The most stressful part of the entire experience was the anticipation. Once the reality of the event (free-falling) took over, the fear vanished.

There is a Zen saying: "Leap, and the net will appear." Those moments right before you do something are the worst, but they are no argument against ripping off the Band-Aid or making that jump. You'll grow your wings on the way down. And the next time you are scared to take that next step, to take a chance, to make a dreaded phone call, or to tell someone no, you'll take the initiative a little bit sooner. You'll start doing the work instead of sitting in the bleachers waiting—suffocated by dread, paralyzed by fear—and wondering, *What if … ?*

Acting on the items that are firmly within your Span of Control can give you back a sense of power in situations where that power is challenged. Even if you feel afraid, anxious, disappointed, or completely screwed over, move quickly from analysis and distraction to your plan of action. Respond. Be intentional. Stay focused on those top three priorities. (Remember that Post-it Note trick? Family, fitness, finances? Meatball, line up, angle of attack? Top three?) Feel the fear and act anyway. Nobody can prevent you from choosing to move forward and be exceptional. You *can* do something specific that can lead to a more positive outcome. Your first move may be picking up the phone or just getting out of bed, but whatever it is, keep moving forward.

ACT DECISIVELY AND TAKE THE INITIATIVE.

Remember that the difference between who you are and who you want to be is *what you do.* It may not be pretty, and it may not come easily. But if you know it to be the right course of action, act decisively and take the initiative.

When making quick decisions or important choices, our goal is to have enough insight to 'automate' some decision making, so our brains can focus on what matters most. Your Span of Control is determined by the things you can, and should, focus on. Everything else is just a distraction.

THINGS *ALWAYS OUTSIDE* YOUR SPAN OF CONTROL:

- **Other people.** The only thoughts and actions you can ever really control are your own. If other people are doing things you don't necessarily care for, guess what? There is nothing you can do about that. Move on.

- **The past.** What's done is done. If you've made mistakes or have regrets (which, goodness knows, we all do), the only thing you can do is make decisions about how they affect your present and your future.

- ***What-if* scenarios.** For every decision you make, there is a resounding *"But what if?"* That will *never* change. While being thoughtful about potential outcomes is certainly a smart and prudent thing to do—it's risk management 101—endlessly thinking of every possible outcome *and then not ever taking action* is not smart. By taking the focus off the uncontrollable variables (other people) and putting it on a more controllable variable (yourself and your decisions and actions), you will greatly reduce your anxiety.

- **World crises.** It's true, friends. Most likely, you will not be able to solve world hunger or find a cure for a plague. It's important to remember there are a lot of unfortunate things going on in the world outside of your control. Now, that isn't to say we shouldn't lend a helping hand but just to say that you cannot independently handle it and change will not happen overnight.

THINGS *ALWAYS WITHIN* YOUR SPAN OF CONTROL:

- *You.* You are the CEO of your own life. Remember the traditional business-meaning of Span of Control: "the area of activity and number of functions, people, or things for which an individual or organization is responsible."[34] It may be impossible to change certain situations, but it is very much possible to change your thoughts, mindset, and perspectives.

YOU ARE THE CEO OF YOUR OWN LIFE.

- *Your* future. What's done is done, but your future is yours for the taking. While life is always uncertain, it is indeed shapeable, and you can do things now that will help you later.

- *Your* actions. What-if scenarios are helpful, and even critical, to planning and increasing your situational awareness. But we can't what-if something to death. That's called analysis paralysis, my friend. In contrast to "what if," "what now" actions are *the* catalysts for changing your circumstances. To have the most influence on your current situation, focus on changing *your* behavior.

- *Your* community. You may not be able to solve world hunger, but you can certainly give your neighbor some lunch. One of the quickest paths away from being overwhelmed and toward taking control is to do good things within your immediate community. You can indeed make a distinct, positive change in the world.

Markets shift, economies change, friends disappoint, family leave—these are external factors that can't be controlled, but remember, you are always in control of how you act and react. While it's okay to be afraid to fail, it is not okay to avoid *trying* to change your circumstances for the better, even just 1 percent.

CREATE A COURSE OF ACTION

When you are at peak overwhelm, it's important to identify *three general everyday things you can do to recenter and refocus* so that you can make the best decision and take appropriate action. These three things are your three go-to actions that you can always have on the back burner when your brain doesn't have the capacity to think as keenly or sharply due to task overload or some other stressor.

What I have seen to be an effective three-step course of action might surprise you with its simplicity:

1. *Gather information* about an opportunity to act, and put that information down on paper.

2. *Interpret the information* to make a list of pros and cons regarding the opportunity.

3. *Move your body* to change your state, then return to the list to make a decision.

This three-step course of action helps with decision-making by moving me past gathering and interpreting information and allowing me to get some "distance" after identifying reasons for and against a decision.

Here's a more specific list:

1. Go for a run

2. Call a trusted friend

3. Drink 32 oz. of water

Whatever three things you choose, they must all be directly within your Span of Control, and they must all be things that you can rely on to get you on a path of clarity.

Write your three go-tos here:

1. _____

2. _____

3. _____

Analysis paralysis happens to the best of us. There are days where problems, issues, to-dos, choices, and big decisions will pile up, and we'll find ourselves feeling buried and stuck. The **MOVE FORWARD WITH COURAGE.** trick is not to linger there. Take a moment to reflect, but don't dwell, wallow, or overthink. *Move forward with courage.*

Contrary to what many people think, courage does not consist of the absence of fear. Courage, rather, is the mastering of fear—feeling the fear and going forward anyway.

It's your inner fortitude that allows you to face danger—to believe in a valuable outcome, to overcome barriers, and to step up and take a chance—even when a situation seems impossible, even when you're terrified. This is *not* the same thing as taking bad risks or showing false bravado. **It is choosing to live with hope, which fuels action, instead of being crushed and paralyzed by your fears and hesitations.**

FOCUS QUESTIONS

- When is the last time you felt analysis paralysis, too stuck to make a decision?

- When is the last time you made a decision, then made a mistake, but learned from it and *kept moving forward*?

- What differences do you notice between the two events you described?

- How can you restructure your day in order to *do* more and *overthink* less?

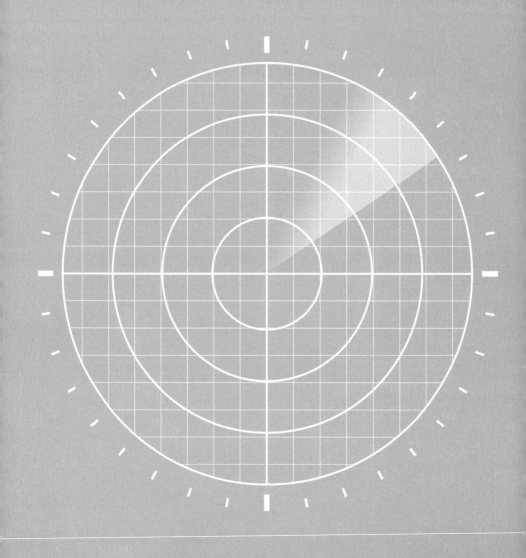

PART III

TAKING CONTROL AND GOING BEYOND

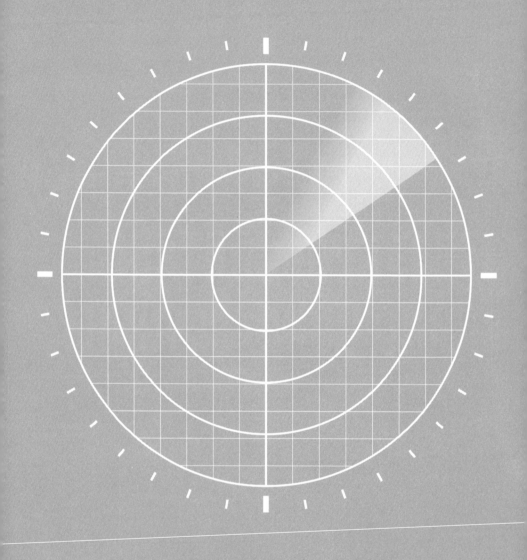

Chapter 8

FOCUS ON
WHAT MATTERS MOST

R owing is a grueling sport, often ranked as one of the top three most difficult on the planet. Everything about it hurts. In fact, it is sometimes described as the only sport that started off as capital punishment. Seriously! In southern Europe, starting in the 1400s, if you were convicted of a crime, you were either executed or sentenced to be an oarsman.

Thanks to Mother Nature, the best water—the flattest—is usually early in the morning, so 5:00 a.m. wake-ups are the norm. And when you are rowing at a competitive level, the pain of getting out of bed in the cold predawn is only the beginning. Maintaining physical coordination in this effort is critical. One misplaced "catch"—dipping your oar in the water—could launch you from the boat. Your hands look as if they've been put through a meat grinder: blisters, calluses, blisters under calluses. Your legs feel as though a million needles are jammed in them. You're sure that either your lungs will explode or you will suffocate from lack of oxygen—whichever comes first. The pain is so intense it scrambles your thinking; every bit of survival logic is telling you to quit. Even your eyes are affected by the effort—your vision goes full-on tunnel.

You are convinced you might die. You're sure there is no way in hell you'll ever make it to the finish line, and yet ... there is the voice inside your head, just loud enough, that tells you not to quit on your teammates.

So *you focus. You persist.*

The summer before my junior year of college, a group of us stayed at school for the summer rowing session. We took a couple of classes, and we trained for the fall racing season. In particular, we were preparing for a prestigious race in Boston—the Head of the Charles—that draws top national and international rowing crews along with hundreds of thousands of spectators. No one outside of our team expected our crew from UW to do well, and for a few legitimate reasons. First, we were a young crew with a gap in experience and seniority. Second, there were upward of forty-five other crews in our one race alone. And third, one of those other crews had just rowed in the Olympics. Seriously? What were our chances?

Being the seasoned college junior that I was, I had learned already the power of establishing a vision to which everybody could orient their day-to-day decision-making. I knew there had to be a catalyzing or compelling idea that would get our team headed in the right direction.

The vision here was simple: we wanted to win at the Head of the Charles.

All we had to do was make our boat faster than the other boats. So every day that summer we asked ourselves as we were training, **"Will this make the boat go faster?"** Everything that we did was in the context of answering that basic question.

If we were going to run stadium stairs, would an extra fifteen minutes make the boat go faster? To our discomfort, manifested in the immense pain we experienced in those fifteen minutes, yes, it would. We would grind out excruciating workouts day after day with a singular goal in mind: winning at the Head of the Charles. Most days it would've been easier to stop.

As all of our friends and pals were ramping up for their nightly college activities, we would have to ask ourselves, "Will this make the boat go faster?" Of course, we came to that answer quickly: no, it wouldn't. Now, I'm not saying I never went out—I did go to the University of Wisconsin–Madison, after all! But I knew, as did my teammates, that how we conducted ourselves socially and the choices we made would directly affect our ability to move the boat faster.

We showed up at the Head of the Charles that October, and our boat swung through that three-mile course with grit, power, practiced precision, and a fierce but quiet determination. At the end of the race, when all finish times were in, we were number one: the top collegiate crew in the nation.

We accomplished this because we kept our goal out front and focused on our Span of Control:

- We identified the top three things we needed to do as a team to make the boat go faster.

- We had a written-down plan for success (our training and race plan).

- We had a communication plan for helping one another through difficult moments.

We identified the things we could control: The intensity with which we practiced, the time spent on the water, time in the weight room, time on the erg, strength tests, what we ate, and the decisions we made off the water. We tracked our workouts, our water time, our downtime, the race plan. If any of us were struggling, we hashed it out—we communicated to support one another.

Focus is an action. And we took action. We did the work; we pursued that goal no matter the obstacles.

Rowing is such a unique sport. **With effort, you get better, but to go fast, it never gets easy.** The sport relies heavily on personal motivation and discipline—the ability to continue on when you feel like you don't have enough air to breathe and the pain is too intense to continue. Also, you can't go it alone. You need training partners to push you (no one's seat or position is ever safe), coaches to give you feedback, and great wingmen—on the team and at home—to whine to about the nonstop pain, show off your blisters, or obsess about your rigging.

The lessons I learned from my time at UW—about persistence, grit, staying calm and focused, and the power of possibility—stay with me to this day.

As Sir Matthew Pinsent, an English rower who has won ten World Championship gold medals and *four consecutive* Olympic medals, shared: "Panic is a bad thing in a rowing boat and never more so than in the stroke seat. Panic makes the stroke rushed and short, both of which are killers to speed … and either you are in and focused, and in it to win, and it takes first priority, or you're not and you can have off all the days you like."[35]

FOCUS IS POWER. DILUTED FOCUS EQUALS DILUTED POWER.

Focus is power. Diluted focus equals diluted power.

Here's the bottom line: think carefully about those things that do not contribute to what you want—and throw them overboard. Get rid of the noise, clarify the complex, and ask yourself: *Will this make the boat go faster?*

Because your brain is always "on" and taking in information, it must constantly choose what to pay attention to and what to filter out and ignore.

—CAREY LOHRENZ

Train Your Brain

Picture yourself in the heart of New York City's Times Square.

At the intersection of Seventh Avenue and Broadway, you'll find an insane amount of flashing neon signs, jumbotrons, and billboards. Towering high-rises surround you. Taxis honk, people yell, music blares. The smell of roasted nuts, hot dogs, and car exhaust permeate the air. You'll be greeted by many cartoon characters—Spider-Man, Elmo, or Elsa—asking if you want a picture with them (for a price of course), and no doubt you'll run into a handful of tourists snapping pictures smack-dab in the middle of the sidewalk.

Woof. It's a lot to take in.

But as we have already learned, our brains have limits, and the frenzied chaos of Times Square can easily cause an overload of sensory information. So does trying to work from home, managing your kids' online schooling, attending that board meeting on Zoom, fending off apathy and overwhelm—not only in yourself but your teammates as well. To overcome all these sensory inputs, the brain uses various filtering mechanisms, broadly referred to by neurologists as "selective attention." Although we may think we are seeing a single comprehensive image, in actuality, we are sampling things, deciding which information is important and interesting and which information is not.

Because your brain is always "on" and taking in information, it must constantly choose what to pay attention to and what to filter out and ignore.

Researchers at Princeton Neuroscience Institute have concluded that our ability to focus is designed to work in bursts of attention rather than uninterruptedly. So while it may seem that you are continuously focused on reading this book, the reality is that you're actually zooming in and out of attention up to *four times per second*. The researchers found that in between those bursts of attention, we are distracted. During those periods of distraction, the brain freezes and scans the room to see if there is something else that might be more important. If there is not, it focuses back on what we were doing.

This means we are *hardwired* to prioritize, and we are, indeed, not designed to sustain task overload or overwhelming amounts of information.

Selective attention comes in two different forms:

TOP-DOWN

Top-down focus is goal and purpose oriented. It's responsible for seeing the bigger picture and uses past experiences to figure things out—like when you're studying for that big presentation or trying to solve a difficult problem.

BOTTOM-UP

Bottom-up focus happens when something suddenly grabs your attention—like those pesky pings, dings, or notifications. You can't help but pay attention to what's happening around you—for instance, when you shift your focus to something more immediate at hand, like a breaking glass or a knock at the door.

Here's the issue: you can't control what kind of focus your brain is using. Despite wanting to stay in top-down, superfocused mode—I mean, wouldn't we all?—

> **HERE'S THE ISSUE: YOU CAN'T CONTROL WHAT KIND OF FOCUS YOUR BRAIN IS USING.**

bottom-up focus is able to override our brain's filters via forces both external (the people and things in our surroundings) or internal (our emotions and beliefs).[36]

To put it another way, there are *sensory* distractions and *emotional* distractions. There is the *outer dialogue* going on at the table next to you in the coffee shop, and there is the *inner dialogue* going on in your own brain.

Let's say that you're trying to buckle down and finally finish a business plan you've been putting off. If your dinging, beeping, ringing phone (a negative external force) is in your periphery *and* you're stressed the heck out (a negative internal force), you're going to struggle to focus and concentrate on getting that business plan done well … if at all.

But there's a flip side to this scenario. If your desk is clean and tidy, you've made the decision to work until noon, and you've put an old-school clock on your desk (all positive external forces), plus you're in a calm and at-ease state (a positive internal force), you are no doubt going to find it much easier to be, *and stay*, focused. Knocking out that business plan? No problem. Top-down focus, here we come.

Here's the catch, though. Forces can also counteract one another—and sometimes the negative forces feel stronger than the positive, especially if the negative force is an internal one.

If your work environment is technology free and your desk is tidy (positive external forces!), but you're anxious about the state of the economy (negative internal force), you could still struggle to stay focused.

Unfortunately, it's not usually the noise of the things around us that keep us distracted but the noise in our own brains. Earplugs, headphones, and moving to a quieter spot can remove the external noise, but what can quiet the internal noise? What can eliminate the problems, pressure, and anxiety that we create for ourselves?

While you can't necessarily control *what kind* of focus your brain is using (top-down vs. bottom-up) you can control *what* you are focusing on. How?

This is where understanding your Span of Control is critical.

Focus or flail. Your choice … #SpanOfControl

FOCUS OR FLAIL. YOUR CHOICE ...

Focused To-Dos

Imagine if you were to dump all your problems, concerns, and emotional distractions out on the table. It might look something like this:

That presentation in two weeks, internet, emails, texts, Instagram, Facebook, Twitter, dog videos, the conversation from last night, I need to go to the gym later, gosh, I still need to send out that proposal, I need to book that flight, the market crash, damnit my babysitter just canceled this week, who is going to watch my kids? I need to do my taxes, am I drinking enough water? Ugh, the election, the disaster overseas last night, oh, I want to see that movie this weekend! Is that picture crooked? Will I be able to afford my kids' college? Wait, there's another thing I have to buy for school? Ten people quit today? Those shoes are how much? I can't believe she said that this morning …

For each of however many distractions you face, put them through the filter of what you *cannot* control (others, the future, what-if scenarios, world problems) and what you *can* and should control (you, your future, your actions, and your community).

Then, looking only at what you can and should control, ask yourself three things:

1. Will this make my Post-it Note?

2. Is this thing *beneficial or important* to the goal(s) I am trying to accomplish *today*? Saving up for your children's college may indeed be a goal worth focusing on, but if you are on a

deadline to get that presentation completed or that business plan written, being distracted by an issue that is not resolvable today is just a distraction getting in the way of accomplishing your goals. Even worthwhile distractions are distractions.

3. Is this thing *controllable right now*? It may be fine that something is *generally* controllable, but is there something you can do right now—this. very. moment.—that would actually resolve or change this concern?

If you were to cross out all of the uncontrollable and unbeneficial distractions, that inner dialogue might look more like this:

That presentation in two weeks, ~~internet,~~ emails, ~~texts, Instagram, Facebook, Twitter, dog videos, the conversation from last night,~~ I need to go to the gym later, gosh, I still need to send out that proposal, I need to book that flight, ~~the market crash, dammit my babysitter just canceled this week, who is going to watch my kids? I need to do my taxes, am I drinking enough water? Ugh, the election, the disaster overseas last night, oh, I want to see that movie this weekend! Is that picture crooked? Will I be able to afford my kids' college? Wait, there's another thing I have to buy for school? Ten people quit today? Those shoes are how much? I can't believe she said that this morning ...~~

What's left?

Presentation, emails, exercise, send the proposal, book the flight.

When you do this, you'll find that there are certain things that are under time constraints and that vary in priority and in the amount of time and effort needed. Some people say to always start with the big stuff first, but I always recommend getting a few little wins under your belt. It's all about prioritization and time management.

1. Just book the damn flight you keep forgetting about. This takes, what ... ten minutes?

2. The proposal has been done for days, and you've been anxious about sending it—just swallow your pride and send it now! Do it! Done!

3. Knock out a few emails. (FYI: The "snooze" button in Outlook and Gmail is a phenomenal tool when it comes to Span of Control. If there is something you need more info on before responding, snooze it until you know you'll have that intel. If it's going to take an amount of time that you do not have today, snooze for a day you know you will have that time.)

4. Now it's time for the big stuff. Block out four or five hours to get some work done on that presentation. Set a specific goal for how much you want to get done, and work until you hit that goal. If you're having a tricky time due to internal forces, try to keep hacking away at it for the amount of time you have delegated.

5. End (or start) your day with some self-care, and be sure to get that workout in. Personally, I am a morning workout person because it kicks my brain into gear and gives me an enjoyable first win of the day. And by the end of the day, I'm just gassed and would rather curl up with Netflix and carbs.

That takes you from twenty things to five and five only (the fewer the better!). The first three can be accomplished in a shorter time span, so once those are knocked out, it really comes down to two things: the big, scary presentation and that workout you never manage to squeeze in. When anxiety creeps in or more things pop up that start to cause overwhelm (and trust me, they always will), go back to asking yourself those two questions:

Is this thing beneficial or important to the goal(s) I am trying to accomplish today?

Is this thing controllable right now?

Then refocus your energy and effort to the (preferably) two things you need to accomplish *right now. Presentation, exercise. Presentation, exercise. Presentation, exercise.*

Direct your time, energy, and resources to solving those challenges that make a difference!

DISTRACTION ELIMINATOR

Make a list of everything that is on your to-do list and on your mind right now. I mean *everything. Just do a brain dump.* So often that thing that comes out of left field as we begin writing our thoughts is the thing that keeps distracting us subconsciously. Make as long a list as needed.

_____

_____

_____

_____

_____

_____

_____

_____

_____

_____

_____

Now, go through the list and ask: *Is this thing controllable **right now?***
> If not, cross it out.

Then ask: *Is this thing beneficial or important to the goal(s) I am trying to accomplish **today?***
> If not, cross it out.

Now write down the things that are left, and be sure to prioritize them based on importance and on what would make you feel less over-whelmed and more clearheaded and excited sooner rather than later. Ideally, there should not be more than five. If there are, more than likely you need to block out time on another day to handle the excess.

_____

_____

_____

_____

_____

_____

_____

_____

Your Not-To-Do List

The plane was about ready to take off when Warren Buffett walked up to his personal pilot of ten years, Mike Flint, and reportedly said, "The fact that you're still working for me tells me I'm not doing my job. You should be out, going after more of your goals."

They chatted a bit about life and career priorities, and Buffett then walked Flint through a simple, quick process that is now known as the 5/25 Rule.

The first thing Warren Buffett asked Flint to do was to list the twenty-five most important goals he wanted to achieve in his lifetime.

Once Flint compiled his list, Buffett asked him to draw a circle around his top five most important goals.

Then Buffett reportedly asked, "Are you sure these are the absolute highest priority for you?"

Flint replied, "Yes."

After the brief discussion, Flint said to Buffett, "Warren, these are the most important things in my life right now. I'm going to get to work on them right away. I'll start tomorrow. Actually, no, I'll start tonight."

Buffett replied, "But what about these other twenty things on your list that you didn't circle? What is your plan for completing those?"

"Well, the top five are my primary focus, but the other twenty come in at a close second. They are still important, so I'll work on those intermittently as I see fit as I'm getting through my top five. They are not as urgent, but I still plan to give them dedicated effort."

"No. You've got it wrong, Mike," Buffett said. "Everything you didn't circle just became your *avoid-at-all-cost list*. No matter what, these things get no attention from you until you've succeeded at those top five."[37]

Saying *no* to things is crucial to optimal focus and unequivocal success. Buffett was advising on how to reach your biggest life goals. But you can apply this rule to help you with smaller, daily priorities as well.

"NO MATTER WHAT, THESE THINGS GET NO ATTENTION FROM YOU UNTIL YOU'VE SUCCEEDED AT THOSE TOP FIVE."

THE 5/25 RULE

Step 1: Write down your top twenty-five goals.

_____

_____

_____

_____

_____

_____

_____

_____

_____

_____

_____

_____

_____

_____

_____

_____

_____

_____

_____

_____

_____

Step 2: Draw a circle around your top five goals.

Step 3: Cross off all the rest.

Focus on your top five goals, and remember to say no to the rest.

Remember this, friends: what you *don't* do determines what you can do. The number of things on your not-to-do list should far outweigh the things on your to-do list. Try to have no more than three things at the forefront of your mind each day, and keep in mind that there are different to-do lists for your day, your year, and your life.

WHAT YOU *DON'T* DO DETERMINES WHAT YOU CAN DO.

Raise the Bar

In my current line of work, I get to meet fascinating people with extraordinary stories of overcoming challenges and great obstacles while still finding a way to create success for themselves and others along the way.

Antonio Neri, CEO of HPE, is one of those people. I had the opportunity to work with his team, and we had several fantastic conversations about their journeys and his. Humble, gracious, and kind, Neri is passionate not only about technology and its potential for making life better but also about the people he works with.

His focus is on serving the customer and then on innovation and creating a culture of high performance and creativity—one that empowers his leaders to make decisions and make them quickly. What seems to come easily to him now—leading, understanding the psychology of people, translating technology-speak to business outcomes, telling stories—was learned through hard work, experience, and focusing on his Span of Control.

Originally born in Italy and raised in Argentina, at just fifteen years old, he was already an engineering apprentice working with the Navy helping to maintain combat vessels. One of those ships, an Argentine light cruiser, the *General Belgrano*, was sunk by a British submarine when the Falklands War erupted. Three hundred twenty-three people perished.

When I had the opportunity to work with his team, Neri recalled what a traumatic experience it was, but also how he was struck by the sense of community and the ways that people looked out for one another during that time of grief and overwhelm.

Focusing on what he could control throughout his life, he worked to earn a degree in engineering and train as a professor of art and drawing. He intentionally sought out mentors and actively accepted "stretch assignments." Originally from Latin America, he also worked in Europe before moving to the United States. He got his start at HP working in a call center, hoping to one day make general manager.

With his engineering background, multilingual skills (he speaks four languages), and a dedication to weaving together the pragmatic and the practical by constantly learning and staying curious, he was able to make an impact with every opportunity.

When we talked together about my idea of Span of Control as both a tool and mantra, Neri's response was enthusiastic: "You have to continually raise the bar and maintain a clear focus on priorities. When faced with challenges and uncertainty, double down on execution and your culture. Yes, ask yourself, your team, 'What's within my Span of Control?'"

Remind yourself and your team of both the challenges and the opportunities that come with uncertainty:

- Mindset is everything: you must stay positive and solutions-oriented.

- Know the specific outcomes you're looking for.

- Execute your purpose, vision, and strategy with urgency.

- Embrace the discomfort.

- Step up and lead during times of uncertainty (**don't wait for an invitation to make a difference**).

- Be dedicated to continuous learning.

- Focus on your customers', clients', and partners' needs—relentlessly.

Neri emphasized how important it was to not only celebrate the team's success and the progress they made but also to keep pushing toward greater success. "Accelerate, accelerate, accelerate. The future belongs to the fast."

> ## "ACCELERATE, ACCELERATE, ACCELERATE. THE FUTURE BELONGS TO THE FAST."

That's why you and your team must work continuously to clarify the complex, figure out what tasks to shed, and make your to-do list a reflection of your most important priorities.

Remember from chapter 5: "If you lose sight, you lose the fight!"

If you lose sight of the most valuable work you should be doing? You are guaranteed to lose the fight. **Remember: Focus is power. If you dilute your focus? You dilute your power.**

FOCUS QUESTIONS

- When do you focus best? Make note of the external and internal factors that could be at play.

- Is there anything on your plate that you can hand off to clear some space?

- Ask yourself: Why do you think you have a hard time saying "no" to certain things?

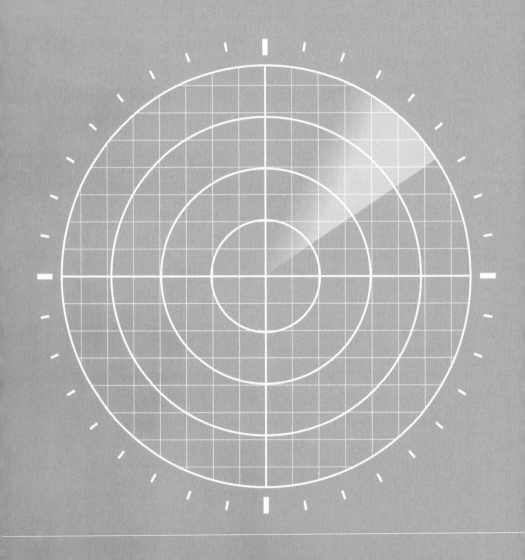

Chapter 9

BIG GOALS AND BIG WINS

knew early on that I would someday be an aviator. Flying was in my blood.

My older brother and I grew up playing with dad's silk maps and flight gear from his time flying in the USMC. We'd perform imaginary feats of daring and skill, pretending to be pilots just like our dad. Given this heritage, my brother and I had no doubt even as kids that we were destined for the cockpit—and we were both right.

The path to a piloting career is a challenge for anyone, no matter how driven and naturally skilled you may be. What I didn't know as a child, though, was that it would require an extra helping of courage from me simply because I was a woman. On top of that, I decided while an undergrad at the University of Wisconsin–Madison that I didn't just want to be any ol' pilot. I wanted to be a naval aviator—a coveted title even among men in the field. For a woman, especially in the 1990s, aiming for that goal seemed silly. Nevertheless, it was all I wanted, and I held that dream tight.

The first step anyone has to take on the path to naval aviation is getting commissioned as a naval officer. For me, the best way to do that was to apply to Aviation Officer Candidate School (AOCS) at the Naval Air Station in Pensacola, Florida.

My brother had attended AOCS, and his example encouraged me. Still, the AOCS application process was intimidating. I applied in the summer of 1990 with no flying experience under my belt. I wasn't an aerospace engineering major; I had earned my BA with a double major in psychology and social work. I wasn't sure how I was going to do on the initial entry exams, which included tests of math skills, reading skills, mechanical comprehension, spatial apperception, and both aviation and nautical information. I was pretty sure that as long as I was prepared and went through the study guides, I would be okay—but there were no guarantees. I knew that even if I got in, only a handful of those who made it to Pensacola would earn those prized aviator wings, and only an extremely small percentage of student naval aviators would go on to become aircraft carrier fighter pilots.

Right around the time I was graduating from college and getting ready to apply, my brother was graduating from AOCS himself. In May 1990, I went down to Pensacola for his graduation and got to meet his friends—all aviation officer candidates like him. One night a bunch of us went out to the Flora-Bama, a legendary beach bar on the Alabama-Florida state line. Naturally, after a few beers, conversation started flowing. I'd been cast in the role of "little sister," and questions flew when these new officers discovered that I, too, wanted to fly. Most of the guys were supportive and thought it was "cool." Some thought I was bat-shit crazy; several of them said things like, "You seem way too nice. Why would you want to do this?" But one guy at the Flora-Bama that night was vehemently opposed to the idea of me becoming a naval aviator.

This was the first time I'd run across somebody my age who truly didn't believe women should be in combat. This new adversary of mine was passionate about his position; he proclaimed that women should be the keepers of the home and family and had no business being in combat. I was shocked. This guy was well spoken and college educated, a friend of my own brother—how on earth could he be such a caveman?

With his statements, the lines in the sand were drawn. We both argued our positions, nearly shouting over the bar noise, and by the end of the night, we had to just agree to disagree on this one point. He was a sweet Southern boy from Louisiana—pure Cajun. His were long-held, ultratraditional views. I could respect that, and I probably wasn't going to change his opinion.

But the bluntness of that opinion left me stunned. How could somebody who didn't even know me or know whether I would be capable of being a naval aviator say, right out of the gate, "You don't belong here"? To me, that just seemed crazy. Women flew in the military in the 1940s, did he not know this?

After all, I wanted to serve my country, just like this guy did! I was drawn to naval aviation and the culture it held so dear—mission before self, a warrior mentality—just like this guy was. I knew the program would be hard enough on its own, but now I had to face a truth: I would have to fight some people on the inside. If the people whom I was supposed to be working *with* were against the idea of me even being there, would it be impossible to make it through the program? Would I have the strength to express my convictions when challenged?

My brother's buddy wasn't the first or only person to give me flak for my dream—far from it. There were several people along my journey to becoming a Navy fighter pilot that would tell me that my goals were unrealistic and my dreams just plain silly. I mean, other people's perceptions of what was possible were definitely not within my Span of Control, but there were days, naturally, when those perceptions really got to me.

THE BIGGER THE GOAL, THE LOUDER THE VOICES OF UNCERTAINTY (BOTH EXTERNAL AND INTERNAL) CAN BE.

Self-doubt will plague us all. Unfortunately, the bigger the goal, the louder the voices of uncertainty (both external and internal) can be. There is a path through that, though.

My internal dialogue was: *ignore the haters, work hard, you'll learn something new regardless of the outcome.*

If you aren't able to shove that hesitancy and those doubts to the side and be bold in your convictions, I promise you those dreams are more than likely never going to come to fruition. Flights go untaken. Books go unwritten. Promotions go unchased. Companies stagnate. Teams dissolve.

Oftentimes we hear people talking about Big Hairy Audacious Goals (BHAGs)—the truly aspirational goals that people say they want to achieve but that can seem improbable. Span of Control is about setting big, *hard* goals, not just SMART goals (Specific, Measurable, Achievable, Realistic, and Time-bound). In today's fast-moving world of innovation and constant change, the hard goals—the ones that push us, challenge us, and give us a sense of progress—are the ones we need to go after. **Research shows us that people are indeed happier when going after the difficult, the audacious, the hard goals.**[38]

This isn't to say that all big, audacious goals are necessarily worth pursuing. Not all dreams are created equal. There are certainly times when the gap between the goal and your current situation is so big that it can be a *demotivating* factor instead of a motivating and inspiring one. The key is to set a big goal with a very clear, step-by-step path for you to achieve it.

The most effective leaders and high performers take the time to do this because they know it's an effective way to identify the most important work they should be doing. Taking that step also helps them prioritize and say "no" to the less important things that threaten to suck away their time.

WRITE THAT BHAG DOWN

In as few words as possible, write your goal here.

YOUR GOAL

_____

_____

_____

_____

_____

_____

With clarity, you can do big things. To clarify your goals, ask yourself the following:

What does success look like?

_____

_____

_____

Why is this important to me or my organization?

_____

_____

_____

Is it possible? Is it possible _for me_?

_____

_____

_____

What are the consequences to me or my organization if I don't achieve this goal?

_____

_____

_____

Once you do that, it's time to define the basics: the _what_, _who_, _why_, _when_, and _how_. For me, that was something as simple as this:

- **What?** To be a naval aviator, a fighter pilot.

- **Who?** (Who are you really doing this for?) Me and my country.

- **Why?** I love seeing the world from the cockpit—35,000 feet above the world—and doing meaningful, world-changing work that is both personally and professionally challenging and fulfilling and with a team that's on a mission.

- **When?** Application deadline: mid-January.

- You'll end with **How**. This is where most people's goals come to a screeching halt. Write your course of action down.

What _____

_____

_____

Who _____

_____

_____

Why _____

_____

_____

When _____

_____

_____

How _____

_____

_____

Big WINS

A goal without a plan is just a wish.
—ANTOINE DE SAINT-EXUPÉRY

You've probably read or heard that quote before. But the more you learn about the man who said it, the deeper it resonates.

Antoine de Saint-Exupéry is mostly known as the author of the beloved novella *The Little Prince*. But he was also known as a great aviator and had what he called "a great thirst to fly" from the very beginning.[39]

He flew valiantly in World War II and survived multiple accidents until his plane disappeared one day over the Mediterranean in 1944 during a reconnaissance mission in advance of Allied troops invading France. Only forty-four years old at the time of his presumed death, Saint-Exupéry managed to cram into his short life what seems like many more decades' worth of achievements. He achieved goal after goal after goal.

Despite failing the entrance exam to the French naval academy, reportedly suffering from depression, and in later years dealing with aviation-related injuries, he not only flew for decades in service to his nation but wrote bestselling novels, renowned journalism, and became a leading voice among the French. He regularly called for unity among his countrymen and urged the United States to join the war effort against the Nazi regime.

Saint-Exupéry was clearly a man of action despite overwhelm, someone who backed up his goals with clear plans—and who followed through.

However, there is something deeper when it comes to this inventive pilot. His life and his stories all point to one sustained message: the importance of keeping a sense of childlike curiosity and lofty vision.

Saint-Exupéry's life stands in sharp contrast to the approach so many of us take to setting goals. We're seduced by the idea of a "fresh start" on January 1, so we make lofty, poorly defined New Year's resolutions—and then we just don't follow through. We're so bad at this that 80 percent of New Year's resolutions fail by February.[40]

We all get a dopamine rush when we set a new goal. It feels good to say where we want to go and to feel the possibility of what might be. We can recreate that New Year's energy at any time of the year by setting a fresh goal, whether it's losing weight, improving our marriage, starting a new creative project, or hitting a revenue target. It's the *follow-through* that's less fun and where most of us fall short.

The main reasons we fail at following through? There are three:

1. Lack of clarity
2. Lack of discipline
3. Lack of accountability

To achieve our most important goals, we must do three things: *get clear, be disciplined, be accountable.*

> TO ACHIEVE OUR MOST IMPORTANT GOALS, WE MUST DO THREE THINGS: GET CLEAR, BE DISCIPLINED, BE ACCOUNTABLE.

GET CLEAR

To be a high performer in any realm, you have to get clear on what you're trying to achieve. Grand ideas aren't enough. Without clarity and focus, they evaporate as soon as something more pressing comes up.

When we're not clear on our goals, we go into react-only mode. We deal with the closest alligator to the boat. We start shooting from the hip, responding to shifting priorities and projects at work, caring for sick relatives, scrolling our days away on social media, thinking *"if only I had … "* We get stuck, we don't muster up the energy to even dare to take a step. That goal we may have thought of or dreamed about fades away in the overwhelm and chaos of the day-to-day. And we end up wasting a lot of time, energy, and money attending to those things that have little to do with what we really want.

What follows? Failed goals, false starts, disappointment, apathy, and yep, more overwhelm.

Mood follows action. You must take action first before waiting to feel like it.

There will *always* be more to do than there is room on your list. That's why you need clearly defined goals as a sorting tool—to tell you what is and isn't truly important (no matter how important it might seem in the moment). Don't confuse your goals with your to-do list.

What do clearly defined goals look like? They look like **WINS.** Clearly defined goals should be:

Written down

Inspiring

Necessary

Supported by an action plan

Written Down: If you want a shot at remembering your *why*, your purpose, in the midst of chaos, write. it. down. Neuroscience research shows us that if you've vividly described and written down or pictured your goal and then put it in a place that's visually easily accessible— stuck on your laptop, your refrigerator, your bathroom mirror—you're almost 1.5 times more likely to be successful at achieving that goal than those who don't.[41]

Writing down or keeping a visual reminder of your goals, your *why*, is a terrific way to give yourself a tenacity boost when the going gets rough. If you've painted a vibrant picture of what success looks like, you can turn to that picture for encouragement when you feel like giving up.

Mood follows action. You must take action first before waiting to feel like it. There will *always* be more to do than there is room on your list.

—CAREY LOHRENZ

During uncertain or tumultuous times, set a goal, map a course of action, and take steps *every day* toward achieving that goal.

In the fighter community flying the F-14, our slogan was "Anytime, baby!" It was embroidered in bold letters on a patch next to a spunky, gun-slinging tomcat mascot and prominently displayed by F-14 pilots. The phrase was originally thrown out as a challenge to the US Air Force's F-15 Eagle to go one-on-one against the F-14 in a dogfight. The F-14 prevailed. "Anytime, baby!" lived on as a powerful, unifying statement of what F-14 pilots and their aircraft were capable of. It wasn't a muddled goal or squishy philosophy or BS corporate-speak feel-good commentary. It was written down, clear, and aimed at action.

Inspiring: When defining and refining your goals, it's important that they actually inspire, stimulate, and fuel you. You'd be amazed how many people's goals aren't really *their* goals but someone else's— whether it's a boss's, a parent's, a child's, a spouse's, a friend's. Working hard at a goal you aren't inspired by will lead you to feel burned out, unmotivated, and inclined to reach for that autopilot button. **Being inspired is how the shift from surviving to thriving takes place.**

Necessary: Just like when filling the Bucket with tasks, when you're creating your goals, you've got to be intentional about what you deem critical, important, or just nice to have. This means setting one big goal as well as determining the smaller proper steps to get there. For instance, if your goal is to lose twenty pounds, fresh food is *critical*, a form of measurement (albeit a scale or just your overall physical well-being) is *important,* and a fancy gym pass is *nice to have*. If your goal is to start a successful podcast, a clear idea, episode plan, and audio equipment are all *critical*, a marketing plan is *important*, superstar guests are *nice to have*. Don't get them confused or you'll get disappointed and discouraged quickly. Focus on the critical first, important second, and think of the nice-to-haves as the cherries on top.

Supported by an Action Plan: First, we write the goal, then we come up with an action plan. Establish your plan, execute the plan—and then if it doesn't work, you have a history to refer back to. You can track things that work and things that don't. Not only do those steps give you an effective sense of control, they also give you a road map to come back to when you get overwhelmed.

WINS (Written down, Inspiring, Necessary, and Supported by an action plan) are the best way to ensure that your goals are not only challenging (i.e., *hard*) but also clear, measurable, achievable, and believable, with the specific results you desire. But that's only the first step. The next—and harder—part is becoming disciplined about working toward them.

GET DISCIPLINED

When we are trying to close that gap between (1) what we say we want and (2) what we are taking actions to do, life gets in the way. It takes *discipline* to stay on track, and *eliminate distractions*. And when we are setting organizational goals, especially ones that require a culture change, leaders will need to be persistent, patient, and diligent when communicating with the team.

When we set goals, most of us never ask ourselves one critical question: Do you currently have the self-discipline, habits, and mental frameworks to be successful, to be a high performer? Or is that an area where you need a boost?

I want you to think about that for a second. Be brutally honest in your answer. Developing the courage to stretch for more demands that you commit to running a marathon, not a sprint.

Do you have the patience to stay engaged with team members, to ask questions, to probe for potential problems? Will you encourage and support your teammates who are pushing and innovating at great risk to themselves? Are you willing to ask for honest feedback? Have you put the processes in place for disciplined execution? Are you currently disciplined in both planning and debriefing? Are you consistently working on developing and growing not only your professional skills but those of your teammates as well? Are you striving to constantly learn (a critical component of both high performance and PTG)?

Achieving a goal requires discipline. Is it easy? No. Will it be worth it? Absolutely.

BE ACCOUNTABLE

Accountability shouldn't feel like a four-letter word. A lack of accountability is one of the biggest shortcomings I see in corporate America today, and it is a morale destroyer. When goals are set, then deadlines are missed, adjusted, or consistently delayed, and then blame for all that is placed on a particular team or division—you'll never be able to build or sustain high performance. When we don't hold ourselves accountable for the work we committed to and when we diffuse the responsibility for performance, morale suffers, performance declines, and the bar is lowered.

Accountability involves having the *tenacity* to keep after a goal and the *integrity* to pursue the goal effectively. It takes courage to be able to work through difficult situations and accept responsibility for the outcome of your decisions. If we say something is important, then we better be following up on it. Know your level of personal responsibility for each thing you take on. Ask yourself: What piece of this do I own? When you learn to take responsibility for results before you place blame, you'll be amazed at what you—and your team—can accomplish.

We hold each other accountable with processes like debriefing, in which we commit to staying open to criticism and feedback and constantly seeking improvement. If someone is lagging behind, we pick them up and provide support.

In every challenge that we faced at AOCS—whether in a helicopter, an A-4 Skyhawk, an F-14 Tomcat, or an F-/A-18 Hornet—when the flight was done, you went back to the briefing room for the debrief and called it like it was. No excuses. No drama. No spin. It was a high-risk, high-reward environment where we were constantly striving to get better.

> WHEN YOU LEARN TO TAKE RESPONSIBILITY FOR RESULTS BEFORE YOU PLACE BLAME, YOU'LL BE AMAZED AT WHAT YOU—AND YOUR TEAM—CAN ACCOMPLISH.

Whether you're assessing performance as a team or individually, the key is to make sure you are generating the right results and meeting performance standards. If there is no assessment or means for holding yourself and others accountable, then an "anything goes" approach can end up leading to disaster. Ask: Did you meet the expectations: Yes or no? And in either case, *why*?

The bottom line is that accountability is about the sincere promises we make to ourselves and others to follow up and follow through.

When you are living life on the razor's edge, you have to know each person's roles and responsibilities. You come to understand that a little bit of backup can go a long way.

In the business world, on teams, and in families, you want everyone involved to feel their interdependency every day—to feel that having one another's back isn't some kind of obligation or burden but instead is a positive, gratifying path to high performance. Especially in difficult and challenging times, teamwork *cannot* mean helping others only if it's easy and convenient to do so.

In the heat of battle amid the everyday chaos of budgets, critical appointments, pandemics, working from home, and navigating an uncertain future, it's easy to lose sight of the big picture. This is when we need our teammates to provide good mutual support. In the Navy, *mutual support* is our phrase for teamwork, and it means that *we back one another up—period.*

How do you delegate critical tasks to a person you don't trust? How will people trust *you* if you don't follow through or if you don't get your tasks done on time, consistently, no matter how menial they may feel? The people around you should not have to follow up a million times to see if a meeting is still on or wonder if today is the day you show up on time. In the Navy, we do what we say we're going to do, and that's that. The same holds true everywhere else: your team is counting on you to do your best.

With every honorable decision you make—whether it's taking accountability for your personal and professional growth rather than playing office politics to get promoted, or stating sales forecast numbers accurately instead of what you think your manager wants to hear, or simply telling a team member, "I'm sorry I made a mistake. How can I make this right?"—you strengthen your integrity and your team's faith in you.

Profits and power are temporary. Great relationships with people who trust you? They're forever.

PROFITS AND POWER ARE TEMPORARY. GREAT RELATIONSHIPS WITH PEOPLE WHO TRUST YOU? THEY'RE FOREVER.

Little Wins

You've set your BHAG, you've clarified the WINS, and you're prepared to sacrifice, roll up your sleeves, and hop to it. But what about the *little wins*?

We all know the old joke about how to eat an elephant ("one bite at a time!"). It may be a chestnut, but it holds a reliable seed of truth. If you start by chunking down your big goal into bite-sized pieces rather than trying to swallow the whole beast at once, you'll supercharge your tenacity and lower your risk of getting discouraged.

During AOCS, some days by the thousandth jumping jack, it felt as though my calves were about to explode. During flight school, by the seventh book plopped in front of me to memorize, it felt as though my brain would melt. During the last pandemic lockdown, when my teams canceled hundreds of events, it felt deflating. And yet, at each turn, in every endeavor, although people would say things like, "I can't do this for three more months!" and despite definitely feeling that way as well, I would take a different perspective: "I can make it to lunchtime," or "I can get through the next five minutes," or "I can do fifty more."

That perspective gives you fuel to keep on pushing just to the next jumping jack, the next book, the next event that might reschedule. It gives you something to focus on in the present rather than an overwhelming goal too far in the future.

Keep in mind that by taking it one step at a time, you haven't lost sight of the BHAG; you've just committed to making it through the next five minutes, the next set of mountain climbers, the next aerodynamics test, the next client event. Those little bites of the elephant lead to your true goal.

The beauty of the one-bite-at-a-time approach is that it's pretty much psychology 101.

Nearly every human is hardwired to desire improvement—to make progress. We all want to get better at the things we do. When you break an otherwise difficult task into more manageable steps, you start to see progress, and that feeds your innate desire for mastery. Once you've stimulated that drive, you're going to have positive reinforcement as you press through challenges. And you'll be better prepared to take on new challenges as well.

The same is true for teams. As a leader, you have the job of being the catalyst who brings your team together, generates buy-in on a shared vision, and offers positive reinforcements along the way. Positivity is uplifting and contagious. It's the oil that keeps the machine of your team running smoothly, ensuring that all the parts work well together. If you can do that by keeping other people's aspirations in view, you'll be able to challenge them to innovate and go beyond "good enough." Even in times of overwhelm, uncertainty, and crisis, remain positive by being forward-looking or by approaching obstacles as opportunities.

Creating smaller winnable goals builds confidence, instills courage, and combats overwhelm. Those smaller goals also give you and your team more opportunity to celebrate the hard work you're doing. And celebration might be among the best way to keep motivated, inspired, and productive.

Remember the enthusiasm you and your friends showed as kids each and every time you did something well? On the basketball court during small-fry games, for example: Make a basket? That calls for high fives. Steal the ball? More high fives, plus some grins and *woo-hoos!* all around.

Celebrating success is a hallmark of high-performing teams. Taking the time to celebrate success builds personal confidence and makes it easier to keep pushing to reach those goals. A 2010 study of soccer players by Gert-Jan Pepping found that the team that celebrated goals with the most enthusiasm typically won the game.[42] No joke. Their enthusiastic behavior was positive motivation. Celebration is contagious and leads to further conquest.

That's a convincing argument for making sure to celebrate your team's successes so that everyone involved feels proud about what they do and realizes they are part of a high-performance family. When you're a well-rounded, unified team, "Well done!" around the office should be a common occurrence, as should acknowledgment of obstacles overcome. Discussions about what the team did right in the past and where it's now headed are expected *and* productive.

At what age do we forget how to celebrate our smaller successes? When did we become too busy? Do we think it doesn't matter anymore? Especially in times of crisis, we may find ourselves just moving on to the next challenge, the next goal, without remembering to enjoy each achievement.

More and more I see people simply forget to celebrate, which means we're forgetting that we are indeed advancing, accomplishing, and progressing toward our goal one little step (or bite) at a time.

Which brings me back to Saint-Exupéry and his story of a grown-up pilot meeting his inner child. Sometimes your dreams can get you higher than logic and realism ever can. You've got to party like the kids on the basketball court. You've got to go for the big win and stretch your creative thinking and your mindset beyond what you (and others) think is possible.

Don't sweat the small stuff—*celebrate it.* Keeping yourself motivated and encouraged with little wins, smaller goals, and minicelebrations not only helps you to be more successful—it's also way more fun.

CELEBRATING WINNABLE WINS

What are some smaller goals you want to accomplish? Think of today, this week, or this month, and name a few smaller goals. These could be as small as "get a car wash" or "book that doctor's appointment I've been putting off." Make a list of some of the doable things, and then put a hard deadline next to each one. Remember, sometimes getting your life in order and knocking off some lingering to-dos is cause for a celebration!

Sample to-do: clean out my closet
Deadline: this Saturday
I'll celebrate by: going to the park with my dog.

To-Do: _____

Deadline: _____

I'll celebrate by: _____

To-Do: _____

Deadline: _____

I'll celebrate by: _____

To-Do: _____

Deadline: _____

I'll celebrate by: _____

To-Do: _____

Deadline: _____

I'll celebrate by: _____

To-Do: _____

Deadline: _____

I'll celebrate by: _____

To-Do: _____

Deadline: _____

I'll celebrate by: _____

FOCUS QUESTIONS

- Do you have a clear BHAG in mind? If so, what is keeping you from pursuing it? If not, what is keeping you from setting one?

- Are you feeling deflated and unmotivated? When is the last time you celebrated an accomplishment?

- Are you willing to make sacrifices for the thing you want to achieve? If so, what kinds of sacrifices are you willing to make?

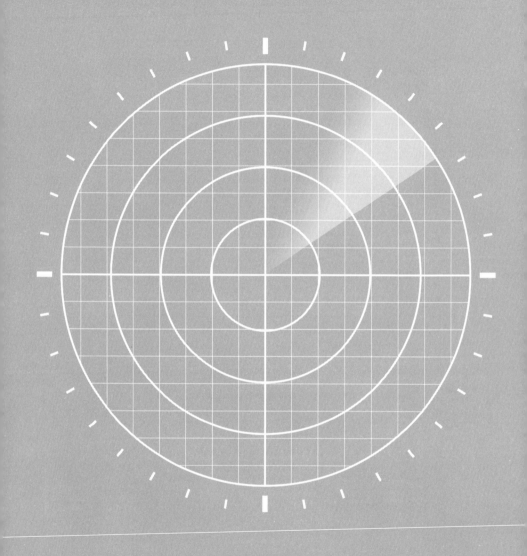

Chapter 10

FORMULATE A FLIGHT PLAN FOR SUCCESS

O n March 25, 2019, passengers boarded a 7:47 a.m. flight from London to Düsseldorf, Germany. Some were headed to see family and friends, and others had full days of meetings scheduled—however, *all* were surprised to land not in the lovely western city of Germany but in … Edinburgh. Instead of heading east, the pilot got lost and flew north, making an unscheduled arrival at 9:00 a.m. in the capital city of Scotland, a full 741 miles from Düsseldorf.

Reportedly, operators gave the pilots and crew the wrong flight plan.

Here's the thing about flight plans: if you don't have the right one, you are wholly unlikely to end up where you want to go.

Funny enough, I have met very few people with *any* kind of flight plan. Most of us are merely passengers, idly watching our lives unfold one day at a time until we arrive at a place of frustration or regret. Instead of the lovely city of Edinburgh, we land in Burnoutown or

Disappointmentville, USA.

While some may plan for their careers, their growing family, or even their next vacation, for most, it never occurs to create a detailed flight plan for their *life*. But without a clear flight plan with mile markers and checkpoints, you can get off track and lose control of where you are going.

In aviation, there is something known as the "drift factor," where things like the current of winds aloft and wind speed can take an aircraft off course. Or there can be procedural drift—when the checklists, policies, or procedures that are available just aren't being used. In our personal and professional lives, drifting usually happens for a handful of reasons:

1. *Unawareness.* Sometimes we drift simply because we don't know what's happening or what's at stake.

2. *Pressure and overwhelm.* Sometimes (and by sometimes, I mean a lot of the time) we take on more than we should. Other times, we are given more than we think we can bear.

3. *Distractions.* Maybe COVID-19 has fundamentally changed your business or work status. Maybe you're in a particularly busy season and are neglecting your physical and mental health. Maybe you're so into that new TV show, you're binge watching it nonstop instead of knocking out that big presentation due next week.

4. *Ego and a lack of humility.* Ego bites us when we think we already know enough to get by and/or we certainly aren't inclined to share our mistakes.

In the cockpit, drifting or getting blown off course can have some pretty deadly consequences—it can lead to full-on plane crashes, running out of fuel, or ending up at the wrong destination. In our living rooms and boardrooms, the consequences can be equally life-altering.

By creating a specific plan (with mile markers and checkpoints) and then following it, your journey to your BHAG will be far easier and less stressful, and your chances of success will be far greater.

If you find yourself drifting, only a clear and focused plan can get you back on track.

> IF YOU FIND YOURSELF DRIFTING, ONLY A CLEAR AND FOCUSED PLAN CAN GET YOU BACK ON TRACK.

Prepare, Perform, Prevail

On day one of flight school, my fellow naval aviators and I learned something that would permanently change the way we operated. It is a deceptively simple process for conducting the business of flying—or conducting any other kind of business, for that matter. In the tiny briefing room at Naval Air Station Corpus Christi, my on-wing (my first flight instructor) made it clear that there is a precise path to high performance. All those hours of classroom instruction, even before ever stepping foot into a Navy aircraft, were driving toward this simple method that would help us plan, execute, and learn from our experiences. I've boiled that process down to an even simpler, straightforward, winning formula: **Prepare. Perform. Prevail.**

In phase one, **Prepare**, you begin by bringing people together to craft a plan for the operation or goal in question. You continue to phase two, **Perform**, by briefing everyone involved in the plan and executing the plan—this is the doing part. And in phase three, **Prevail**, you come together to debrief—to analyze how things went and consider how you can do it better next time.

Right from the start it was clear that we were expected to strictly adhere to that process. It became so fundamental to the way we worked that missing even part of one would cause stress, a feeling that the oversight would definitely come back to bite us. After implementing the process in our daily operations, we came to understand why it received so much emphasis. It provided a way for us to operate at our highest level of performance and to keep learning and improving with every success—and every failure. It helped us achieve sustainable results in a situation where an error by any part of the team, from top echelon to lowest rung, could mean loss of life.

Today, many years since I graduated flight school, I still adhere to the prepare, perform, prevail process. It is a game changer, and if you learn to apply it consistently, it can help you take back control of your life and hit all those goals—both big and small.

You can have the grandest vision ever, but if you can't execute effectively—if you don't have a plan for doing something—then all that effort is worthless.

Prepare, perform, prevail allows you to identify greater opportunities for action in an unpredictable environment. This dynamic process will help make the seemingly impossible possible. It will allow you to execute your steps effectively, adapt and adjust quickly, and manage risk. (Naval aviators are world-class risk managers; few other professions in the world take risk as seriously as we do.) Crucially, it will help you strengthen that growth mindset—when you see failure as a learning opportunity, your fears of it start to dissipate and your courage increases.

Having a straightforward process, a mental model, in place is the heart of Span of Control.

Feelings of overwhelm, anxiety, and stress mellow because by knowing what needs to happen and when, you can course-correct as needed rather than be distracted by every little thing going wrong.

You can have the grandest vision ever, but if you can't execute effectively—if you don't have a plan for doing something—then all that effort is worthless.

—CAREY LOHRENZ

In response to overwhelm and distress, the mental model, the framework, helps us understand the world, says, "This is how you do it. Let's go."

Meatball, line up, angle of attack.

Catch, locate, throw.

Prepare, perform, prevail.

Are you starting to see a pattern here?

They're all mental models, the simple and straightforward frameworks or scripts we talked about in chapter 7 that allow us to make better decisions quickly while also managing risk, stress, and pressure. They're the simple tools we can fall back on to rapidly sort through complex information while simultaneously uncovering and identifying potential dangerous blind spots that might otherwise destroy our performance, our businesses, or our lives.

When the challenges we find ourselves facing feel unsolvable or overwhelming, having these time-tested models allow us to reframe what's challenging as conquerable. They keep us focused on what's within our Span of Control, which helps us keep moving forward and making progress on those things we've identified as most important *to us.*

Having a keen sense of your Span of Control and having a three-part process in place gives you a road map, shows you the most pressing items, and helps you attack them. The prepare, perform, prevail process lights the path ahead, offering a straightforward mechanism to help everyone constantly improve.

This process works for anyone and any team, trust me—whether you are CEO of your company or CEO of your household, there's no task too big or too small for this formula. I've used prepare, perform, prevail with one of the largest utility companies in the United States, within all of the channels of the worlds' largest IT company, with high-performance athletes, and with executives around the globe, and I use it all the time with my kids—before every volleyball game, basketball game, or motocross race.

Recently, I worked with a Fortune 500 telecommunications company, in a market that was changing rapidly, with increased competition and increased selling complexity. Their sales force was being asked to do more and know more (sound familiar?), and they needed help. Our goal was to get the team together, plan, and then turn that strategy into action to accelerate business results.

By walking through the prepare, perform, prevail process, we were able to better understand their customers' business challenges and to discover new and expanded opportunities. We created strategies and execution plans to accelerate sales performance and to enable the sales force to think bigger, analyze the data, take bold risks, and act more strategically as partners to their customers instead of being viewed as "just a vendor."

This whole process created a greater understanding of the roles all the team members played, from the C-level executives to business unit leaders to frontline managers, and to individual contributors. From there, it became possible to put a plan in place that would help them achieve their strategy and the company's realistic goals, with benefits to everyone on the team, both personally and organizationally.

Running through this framework allowed for much greater buy-in, and within sixty days, there was measurable positive impact on both the salespeople's individual performance and compensation and the company's overall financial performance.

Summarizing her personal experience, one telecom director shared, "I started the program thinking I understood our strategy, but I left with a greater sense of purpose, an actionable plan, and a feeling of strong commitment from the team—that we were going to actually make this happen. And we did."

The impact was striking.

Never underestimate the value a simple plan can have on *your* successful execution. It can help you identify what's under your Span of Control, make better decisions, convert those decisions into actions, and accelerate performance results.

PREPARE. PERFORM. PREVAIL.

It is:

- **Effective**. We wouldn't use it in fast-moving, dynamic environments where lives are on the line if it didn't work.

- **Replicable**. When the framework is repeated, it achieves consistent results.

- **Scalable**. It can easily be expanded from use by individuals to use by teams of any size.

The best part? When spectacularly pinched for time or in a moment of crisis, you can convert it into a mere thirty-second focus exercise:

- What's the objective?

- What are we going to work on?

- What could get in our way?

See you at the finish line! Straightforward. Boom! Done.

Phase One: Prepare

Dwight Eisenhower once said, "In preparing for battle I have always found that plans are useless, but *planning* is indispensable." Ah, a man after my own heart. Too often, we have a vision in our minds and the BHAG in our hearts, and then we just start executing. That misses the crucial step: the phase where you prepare by creating the plan. Brick by brick. Step by step. Milestone by milestone.

I want to be clear: planning is *not* the same as setting the goal. Planning is looking at threats and resources and identifying the necessary steps that clearly take you toward the goal. Planning relies on how you define success—what things should look like when the smoke clears—but it is not the same thing as naming or defining that end result.

There's a reason for keeping them separate, and it has everything to do with Eisenhower's remark. Once you start to engage—whether this means you are airborne, in your manufacturing facility, writing the novel, or launching a new business plan—things change. They always do. We may have the goal in mind and clearly written down. But the reality is you need a clear and concise action plan to come back to when you get off track or when problems arise.

> PLANNING IS *NOT* THE SAME AS SETTING THE GOAL. PLANNING IS LOOKING AT THREATS AND RESOURCES AND IDENTIFYING THE NECESSARY STEPS THAT CLEARLY TAKE YOU TOWARD THE GOAL.

We've learned that the best quarterbacks dedicate time to planning in order to execute effectively under pressure; the same is true for medical professionals, musicians, and businesses.

If you've taken the time beforehand to think through possible scenarios and potential threats and obstacles, your chances of responding successfully to change are greatly improved—even if the plan isn't perfect, which it will *never* be, and even if the obstacles are not quite as you imagined.

When we are leading through times of chaos and uncertainty, our goal should be to build the capacity to adapt, to be responsive to an ever-changing environment. By taking the time to plan, to run through simulations, you'll empower everyone by increasing everyone's level of situational awareness and defining expectations clearly while also building shock absorbers into the system.

In chapter 7, I pointed out that you will not always have 100 percent of the information you need. Things change. Time keeps marching on. And 80 percent information is "good enough" to start taking action. The same is true here. Don't let determining your plan keep you from moving on to implementing it. Start executing your good-enough plan so you are not at the mercy of an environment that is outpacing your plan.

START EXECUTING YOUR GOOD-ENOUGH PLAN SO YOU ARE NOT AT THE MERCY OF AN ENVIRONMENT THAT IS OUTPACING YOUR PLAN.

The best way to develop a comprehensive plan time and again, no matter the mission, is to use a checklist. Naval aviators use checklists for everything, which ensures effective execution of even the most routine tasks: preflight, starting our jets, taking off, landing. We want to make sure no critical tasks are missed or dropped. Our strike-planning checklist is twelve pages long! We are human; we forget things—sometimes even the really important things. But not when we use a checklist.

You probably don't need a twelve-page checklist; instead, you can adopt the one we use for our day-to-day flight planning. The following is an example of this tactical planning checklist. You'll recognize some of the entries from our work in earlier chapters. From Wall Street to Wichita, from conference table to dining table, this works.

TACTICAL PLANNING CHECKLIST

1. *Establish the mission objective.* Ask "What does this goal look like at the end state?" The objective should be clear, measurable, achievable, and worthy of your time.

2. *Ask "Has anyone ever done this before?"* You want to find lessons already learned so you don't make the same mistakes. Repurposing knowledge can save time, energy, and money.

3. *Analyze resources versus threats.* What assets do you have that might aid in achieving success? What are the greatest threats or risks that stand between you and your goal? Be specific. Do *not* say, "Oh, that'll never happen ... " Map it out. Consider it.

4. *Map out the "launch plan."* What is your course of action? What steps will you take to achieve success?

5. *Ask "What if?"* Plan for contingencies—surprises, risks, weaknesses, lack of funding, too few people, resources, etc.

6. *Involve a "red team."* Remember this from chapter 5? Get someone or some group of trusted friends who are not involved in the planning process to poke holes in what you've laid out.

7. *Plan to debrief.* This is always part of preflight planning. If you don't schedule the feedback (the debrief) up front, chances are slim that you will actually follow through.

Make decisions more confidently, by reviewing your plans often. Take a hint from TOPGUN: the legendary fighter weapons school reviews its flying and training plans *daily* to stay on track.

Phase Two: Perform

Once you have prepared effectively, it's time to put away fear and doubt, and just *do*. Great execution will depend on your ability and your confidence to jump in and adhere to your plan, making adjustments as necessary.

Don't be afraid to have that goal, that objective, right smack in front of you during this phase: print it out, tape it to a wall, your computer, your desk, use Post-it Notes, get the tattoo, *whatever it takes*—but keep that goal in front of you to keep it top of mind.

Critical enablers of successful execution include:

- Your mindset (your commitment to the purpose and belief in the strategy, paired with urgency).

- Your team alignment to the strategy (you are the catalyst for recognizing the necessary actions for success).

- Your capabilities (your essential skills: leadership, decision-making, professional acumen/knowledge/expertise, continual learning and skill development, and communication).

I've pointed out before that for a fighter pilot, speed is life. You must make decisions quickly, take the initiative, and push the envelope or you will be left behind. As necessary as planning is, we can't extend that phase of the process, overthinking things and getting stuck in analysis paralysis. We prepare thoroughly so that we have no reason for holding back. We have to execute despite fear of failure. As hockey superstar Wayne Gretzky reminds us, "You miss 100 percent of the shots you don't take."

Beginning to execute the plan guarantees that you'll start encountering those contingencies you (hopefully) planned for, but there will always be ones you didn't foresee. This is where your preparation and having those straightforward mental models ingrained helps you manage the overwhelm, the changing environment, the uncertainty and complexity.

To the extent that you are able to rapidly shift from problem to solution, your chance of success will increase.

There will be human error too. We all make mistakes, even the most highly trained professionals among us. More than 80 percent of all civilian and military aviation mishaps are due, at least in part, to pilot error.[43] That means it's also part of the perform phase to expect that you *will* have blunders and slipups along the way. The key to sustaining and improving performance is to not beat yourself up over it. Instead, give yourself a little grace, expect to learn.

> **TO THE EXTENT THAT YOU ARE ABLE TO RAPIDLY SHIFT FROM PROBLEM TO SOLUTION, YOUR CHANCE OF SUCCESS WILL INCREASE.**

Phase Three: Prevail

You've now prepared and performed—but does that mean you're done? Far from it! In fact, you could argue that the third and final phase in the prepare, perform, prevail process is the most critical. The heart of this third phase is the debrief, where you review the first two phases, assess what went right and wrong, root out mistakes, and identify lessons learned that will help you improve performance and prevail into the future.

You can't simply pay lip service to the importance of continuous learning without scheduling and taking seriously both individual and team training, education, and performance review. We can't just tell our teammates to work harder, smarter, and faster; they are already rowing as fast as they can. We need to take it a step further by ensuring that they can adapt and by providing the space and the trust to learn and innovate—that's how the magic happens!

If you rationalize skipping the debrief—"I'm too busy," "My team knows what went wrong," "We don't have time for this," "We'll talk about this in ninety days, " "My team doesn't like confrontation"—or when ego gets in the way, you are literally killing your ability to adapt.

Set those excuses, and your ego, aside. Top performers *must* be able to set ego aside and be able to communicate with their teammates. When you start to feel entitled to respect because of your position— and when you no longer feel the need to ask for input from your teammates—the consequences can be catastrophic.

Whatever industry or team you are a part of, whether you work in a patient-care setting, run your own business, are the VP of channel partners, are a coach, or you're in the financial services industry—the prevail step is not just necessary, it's your secret weapon to ensure high performance.

One of the biggest shifts happening across the globe is digital transformation paired with innovation. So many companies I'm working with right now are struggling to get their minds (and resources) around massive amounts of data. Those that can aggregate, understand, and leverage that data will go farther faster than those who don't. The only way to seize those opportunities is if teammates are able to learn from the insights gleaned from that data—and flip those into strategy and then action.

Being able to develop a culture of learning, smart risk-taking, and collaborative teams that can adapt, be creative, and share lessons learned leverages your team's collective brainpower and will give you a distinct competitive advantage.

In the Navy, the debrief process has been refined over hundreds of thousands of hours and decades of flying. Examining the results of planning and performance has saved countless lives and dramatically

Being able to develop a culture
of learning, smart risk-taking,
and collaborative teams
that can adapt, be creative,
and share lessons learned
leverages your team's collective
brainpower and will give you a
distinct competitive advantage.

—CAREY LOHRENZ

reduced the military aviation mishap rate. Not only that, but it allows for rapid improvement among both the current and the next generation of pilots.

You'll recall that back in chapter 5 I mentioned the US Navy Blue Angel debriefs in which every maneuver of a flight is dissected in detail immediately following each and every flight (the details get murkier the longer you wait). Debriefing is *that* critical. We *must* review the details of our performance every time we fly in order to stay alive and improve.

THE POWER OF THE DEBRIEF IS THAT YOU LEARN FROM PURPOSEFULLY UNCOVERING THE MECHANICS OF SUCCESS AND OF FAILURE.

The power of the debrief is that you learn from purposefully uncovering the mechanics of success and of failure. It's both parts training *and* education; we are dealing with known factors while preparing to deal with future unknowns. The criticisms can be brutal, but they are not about ego or deflection, and they are not about blame. Instead, their purpose is to increase both self-awareness and situational awareness and then to make us more capable of applying lessons learned moving forward.

Never forget that it is just as important to debrief successful events as failures. Why? Even if you manage to execute your plan well, there's always something that could be done better, more effectively, more efficiently. **We never want to leave success to chance.** If you just got lucky, that could be disastrous for the next person to fly that mission; you don't usually get lucky twice. So you must take the time to identify what worked, as much as what didn't, and *why.* No matter where you are on the success spectrum, debriefing after execution—assessing how the previous phases went and identifying the takeaways—is how you protect yourself in the future and how you create a growth mindset that never stops learning.

Unknowns and uncertainty are never going away. In rapidly changing situations, the people who can move through the relevant decision-making cycles more quickly and effectively than others, who can focus on their Span of Control, have a greater chance of success.

DEBRIEFING

Give debriefing a try right now. Focus on one activity from today, and answer the following questions:

1. What was supposed to happen?

2. What actually happened?

3. Why were there differences?

4. What can you learn?

5. How can you incorporate that lesson into execution next time?

For almost one hundred years now, thousands of people have been attempting to climb Mt. Everest with various rates of success. Around six thousand people have successfully made the entire round trip, but hundreds have died in the attempt. Climbers who go beyond that initial "Let's do this!" excitement and who study, respect, and share the lessons learned from factors like weather, snow conditions, avalanche risk, physical fitness levels, fatigue, securing an experienced Sherpa, the descent from summit—those climbers have a greater chance of success. In fact, with that investment in preparation, the probability of a successful climb doubled in 2006–2019 compared to 1990–2005.[44]

My great friend Alison Levine served as team captain of the first American Women's Everest Expedition. She has climbed all Seven Summits (the highest peak on every continent) and has skied both the North and South Poles. No matter the particular journey that she's on, she debriefs with her team at the end of every day.

Alison knows well that she must gather data on the route, on team members' health and ability to perform in extreme conditions, on how much food and fuel were consumed and remain, or on wind and temperature forecasts. Debriefing each of those things is a matter of survival.

In our personal and professional lives, it may not always seem that by debriefing we are also asking the question "How will we survive?" But isn't that essentially what we need to be thinking about? Especially in times of overwhelm and crisis?

Here's how Alison puts it: "At the end of a long day on the route, you're completely exhausted, and your body has been drained of every last bit of energy. So the first thing you have to do is take care of yourself, and that means focusing on the top things you can control: your calorie intake, your hydration, and getting warm. If you do not pay attention to those things, you risk altitude sickness, dehydration, hypothermia, and frostbite. You have to stay healthy in order to perform well and to be a strong contributor to your team."

My question to you is this: What are the things you need to debrief at the end of each day—whether for work, for your family, for whatever activities and organizations you are involved in, for your health and well-being, or for your survival?

Are you really willing to leave those things to chance?

DEBRIEF : DO NOT LEAVE SUCCESS TO CHANCE

Even knowing that the goal is to improve performance, people still avoid the debrief because they *fear their performance being assessed*—whether by themselves, their "enemies," or—perhaps most especially—by the people on their dream team. But if your goal is to achieve the goals you're shooting for, the debrief is a powerful tool that can *actually save you time in the long run* by preventing execution errors.

Debriefing well takes deliberate practice. Take the time to process at the end of each project, especially after an unexpected obstacle or when you find yourself feeling less than in control. Trust me, it's worth the time, no matter how busy you are. Taking the time to improve actually *gives you time back* in the end by reducing all of the execution errors and firefighting.

Debriefing is not about *who* is right but *what* is right.

Your Flight Plan

The goal of prepare, perform, prevail is to maximize your performance.

The uncertainty of life can often take you to places you didn't necessarily sign up to go. Turbulence can get bumpy, even nasty. Having a plan to prepare, perform, and prevail puts the power back in your hands and reminds you what *is* within your Span of Control.

When the winds of change shift, you can always come back to your flight plan. When drift occurs and you find yourself burned out, overwhelmed, and under pressure, there is nothing more empowering than remembering what you wanted when you were at your most inspired and determined, and revisiting the plan you devised for achieving it.

You are the CEO of your life. You can choose to prepare, perform, and prevail, or you can choose to overthink, do nothing, and fail.

A clear plan gives you that crystal-clear path to execute and adjust as necessary, all the while allowing you to focus on your Span of Control to maximize your performance, to learn, and to improve. This is so important that I want to encourage you to take a stab right now at plotting your flight plan for success.

YOU CAN CHOOSE TO PREPARE, PERFORM, AND PREVAIL, OR YOU CAN CHOOSE TO OVERTHINK, DO NOTHING, AND FAIL.

I've dedicated a page per step right here for you to think it through. If now is really (honestly) not the time, go ahead and set a reminder on your calendar. Maybe it's next Saturday morning 7:00 a.m. to 9:00 a.m. that you can dedicate to spending the necessary time. Whenever it is, block it out, and do not schedule over it. Remember that once you've written down your plan, you can always come back and refine it.

Ready? Let's do this.

ESTABLISH THE MISSION OBJECTIVE

The goal:

_____

_____

_____

_____

What will it look like at the end? (Clear, measurable, achievable, and worthy of your efforts.)

_____

_____

_____

_____

By when will you achieve this goal?

_____ / _____ / _____

How often will you review this goal? What mechanism will you use? What will success look like?

_____

_____

_____

_____

HAS ANYONE EVER DONE IT BEFORE?

Create a list of the names of other people who have done what you want to do or something similar to what you want to do. Find lessons already learned so you don't make the same mistakes. Leveraging others' experiences, insights, and knowledge can save you time, energy, and money. Read their bios online, read any books or articles they may have written or interviews they may have done.

Do not skip this research stage.

Name: _____

Entity/Company: _____

Questions to research: _____

_____

Name: _____

Entity/Company: _____

Questions to research: _____

_____

Name: _____

Entity/Company: _____

Questions to research: _____

_____

RESOURCES VS. THREATS

Take stock of what you have and what you lack. Do you have the time but lack the capital? Do you have the funding but lack the insight? Do you have the contacts but not the energy? What are the greatest threats that stand between your team and success?

Consider external realities and internal limiting beliefs that may hold you back. Don't overthink it, just take stock and write it down. Then, next to each of the obstacles, write down a possible way to overcome it. Be specific. Map it out.

Assets: _____

_____

_____

_____

Obstacles: _____

_____

_____

_____

Ways of overcoming obstacles: _____

_____

_____

_____

LAUNCH PLAN

What exact steps do you need to take in order to get where you want to go? Be thoughtful and strategic about each step, and always go back to your main objective if you find yourself drifting.

Keep it simple, and give yourself deadlines.

Action Step 1: _____

Deadline: _____

Action Step 2: _____

Deadline: _____

Action Step 3: _____

Deadline: _____

Action Step 4: _____

Deadline: _____

Action Step 5: _____

Deadline: _____

Action Step 6: _____

Deadline: _____

Action Step 7: _____

Deadline: _____

WHAT IF?

Plan for contingencies—surprises, risks, weaknesses, lack of resources, etc. Thinking about potential worst-case scenarios can help us prepare for undesired surprises and not be debilitated by them when they do come. This is basic risk management. Don't skip this step.

Possible Risks: _____

_____

_____

Potential Weaknesses: _____

_____

_____

Possible Problems: _____

_____

_____

Potential Surprises: _____

_____

_____

RED TEAM

Write the names of your Red Team—people who are not themselves involved in the planning process and who can help you find any glaring problems or inconsistencies, missed opportunities, complacencies, or ignored threats. If you can include someone from the has-anyone-done-it-before? list, that will likely be a good person to have in your corner, but a good, encouraging mentor or wise friend is just as important.

_____

_____

_____

_____

Then call that team into action. Have them gather 'round or, alternatively, send them the sheets you've filled in up to this point, and have them give their input. Write down any and all notes. Look for consistency in their feedback because that's likely where you'll see important patterns.

_____

_____

_____

_____

Debrief

If you don't schedule the debrief up front, chances are slim that you will actually follow through. Set aside a specific date and time. If it is a personal goal, review your progress daily. If it's a business plan, project or goal, plan to debrief immediately following completion.

When debriefing is performed regularly, preferably face-to-face (although via telephone or videoconference works well too), it keeps the organization focused on learning and continuous improvement. Whether you are debriefing a go-to market plan, a sales plan, or a product rollout, the debrief is crucial for analyzing not only your execution but how effective and well understood your plan was.

> REMEMBER, THE DEBRIEF IS NOT ABOUT *WHO* IS RIGHT, IT'S ABOUT *WHAT* IS RIGHT.

Remember, the debrief is not about *who* is right, it's about *what* is right.

When you debrief, begin by asking these questions:

1. What was supposed to happen?

2. What actually happened?

3. Why were there differences?

4. What can we learn?

5. How can we incorporate that lesson into execution next time?

Once you've finished debriefing, always wrap with, "I've made these mistakes, and I can fix them."

FOCUS QUESTIONS

- If you haven't written down your flight plan, what is keeping you from preparing?

- What specific regular activities will move you closer to your goal?

- What milestones will you hit along the way?

Chapter 11

COMMUNICATE TO ALIGN AND ACCELERATE

W e stand in awe on Pensacola Beach, watching the US Navy Blue Angels soar overhead as several gleaming planes fly in perfect alignment making diamond patterns, finger-four, or the classic V-formation across a clear blue sky. But it's more than just a stunning demonstration of skill and prowess. Turns out those formations have a purpose, one that we happened to have taken from our feathered friends.

Ever seen a flock of geese heading south for the winter and flying in a V-formation? As each bird flaps its wings, it creates what is called an *uplift* for the bird immediately following. By flying in a V-formation, the whole flock adds at least *71 percent* greater flying range than if each bird flew on its own. When a goose falls out of formation, it feels the drag and resistance of trying to go it alone and quickly gets back into formation to take advantage of the lifting power of the bird in front. When the goose in the front gets tired, it rotates back, and another goose flies point.

And what about all of that honking? Have you ever noticed that the honking is louder in the evening? Well, it turns out that geese honk to encourage those up front to stay accelerated as the day wears on and their wings get tired. When a goose gets sick or is wounded and falls out of formation, two other geese fall out with that goose and follow it down to lend help and protection. That's my personal favorite detail; it feels as if it was taken right out of the Navy's code of conduct. Those two geese stay with the fallen goose until it can fly or until it dies. Only then do they launch out on their own or with another formation to try to catch up with their group.[45]

Share a Common Goal

It's no surprise that the most famous wingman is Mav's RIO, "Goose," from *Top Gun*. A perfect nickname, considering that if we all would have as much sense as a goose, we would understand that sharing goals and having a sense of community can get us where we want to go a lot more efficiently.

TRAVELING ON THE LIFT WE PROVIDE FOR ONE ANOTHER IS BOTH SMARTER AND SAFER THAN GOING IT ALONE.

Traveling on the lift we provide for one another is both smarter and safer than going it alone.

Your flight plan involves others, even though it's on you to step up and be the leader for making it to your destination. Whether it's your employees, your family, or your running club, you still have the power to align your team and accelerate toward your goals during times of crisis and uncertainty. Even though the inclination may be strong to break out of formation during a trying period, it's flying together that is likely to keep all of you heading in the right direction.

Times of crisis not only challenge our ability to direct ourselves to be productive and forward-looking, but as we know, they also threaten our relationships with our teams and support systems. When you're struggling to get your own act together, it can feel as if it requires superhuman effort to focus on shared goals and even more effort to get and give the necessary feedback that's at the heart of accountability.

When we're overwhelmed and our situations are uncertain, how do we tap into shared goals and values to not just stay on track but actually accelerate our performance?

There will be times when it takes more than a clearly stated vision to keep the team, unit, or organization functioning—even solvent. It'll take action and remembering that you are the catalyst.

Right before the pandemic hit, I was fortunate to work with the Clorox company, a multinational manufacturer of both consumer and professional products. You may be quick to recognize the company name as it relates to bleach, but they also have an enormous line of other household products: Glad bags, Kingsford charcoal, Brita water filters, Burt's Bees, Hidden Valley, and so much more.

What was fascinating to me about this team of high performers is that they saw themselves not only as innovators from an R&D perspective but also as innovators within their supply chain.

And boy, did that ever turn out to be an advantage. In March 2020, demand surged by over 500 percent as everyone around the world was trying to get their hands on bleach and disinfecting wipes. Manufacturing became more challenging, the supply chains were disrupted, and the company had to move very quickly to ramp up production to meet consumer needs. In addition to explosive demand for Clorox wipes came a huge demand surge for Glad trash bags, Kingsford charcoal, and Hidden Valley Ranch—apparently key consumer work-from-home survival necessities in addition to toilet paper.

They were able to keep manufacturing lines moving and supply chains operating by clearly communicating both their needs and their shortfalls to their partners. This allowed not only their immediate supply chains to adapt quickly but also facilitated adaptation within the supply chains that *their* supply chains depended on.[46]

Teamwork. Trust. Mutual support. That's what led to their success.

When we work in volatile environments, gaining alignment will take more time, and yes, even more effort. Work to identify your shared goals, and *acknowledge them to one another*. This isn't about delegating or commanding. Today's problems and challenges are way too complex and change too frequently to think that one person's leadership style alone will make things work. With a shared vision and mutual accountability, you can empower leaders at all levels to step up and take charge.

Being clear about what you hold in common makes it easier to get and keep each other on track. Jointly refer back to your plans; ask for feedback from your board members, colleagues, channel partners, vendors, mentors, and friends; gather insights that will inspire you to keep growing and going. You know by now, I hope, that in addition to accountability, staying on track requires continuous learning and self-reflection.

There is no life hack, and there are no shortcuts. Success does not magically happen—we have to plan for it and then consistently adhere to that plan. Only by doing so, and then taking the time to debrief together to figure out what's working and what's not, can you reasonably expect a measure of success.

Something we all struggle to remember is that when the flight gets more difficult and our wings get tired, it's consistent, honest communication among team members that keeps the flock accelerated and on course.

It's absolutely within your Span of Control to communicate with all those in formation with you—whether that's your team, your employees, your audience, or your own family and friends. And the goal of that in-flight communication should be to empower those crucial people—your C-suite, managers, employees, or your own kids—to make *good* decisions and help actualize the goal out front.

You *can* help those that you depend on to be equally energized and enthused by the idea of staying focused on a shared goal. You *can* keep everyone in formation amid chaos and uncertainty.

> YOU *CAN* KEEP EVERYONE IN FORMATION AMID CHAOS AND UNCERTAINTY.

Mantras and mottos like "embrace the suck" and "hack the clock" are all quick and easy-to-remember phrases that unite, solidify, and simplify some of the complex series of actions that make the military effective, efficient, and *connected*. **When we have a shared framework to operate from, we can make better decisions more quickly.**

So let me give you one more mental model for your toolkit: *Aviate, Navigate, Communicate* (you might remember it from the story of Capt. "Fface" Slater's barricade in chapter 3). This is another three-step process we learned on day one of flight school, and it's a simple process used in times of crisis.

1. **Aviate.** When all goes to hell, you just need to aviate—just fly the airplane. You have to maintain control, get the plane stable, and keep it safe. Without this first step, nothing else really matters. Similarly, in business, when a crisis pops up and people feel overloaded, the first thing you must do is slow down and make sure the team is stable, safe, and operational. Often when we are panicked, we get "time compressed"—time seems to speed by, out of control. Focus on what matters. Maintain control. Fly your airplane.

2. **Navigate.** Only once things are stable do you figure out where you're headed. Doesn't have to be perfect at first—just get the nose pointed in a safe direction. In a crisis, once you've got a sense for the stability of things (or at least an idea of how quickly things are coming unglued if they're truly unstable), you must set a course for action: Where are you going from here? Remember the plan you spent time creating? Review those what-ifs, those contingency strategies. What's the solution? Who can help you? The key here is to stay s-l-o-w-e-d d-o-w-n. The time you spend in deliberate assessment will pay off as you resume navigating forward. I've worked with a lot of executives who are dealing with a crisis and have seen them pull out of a nosedive by slowing things down for a couple of hours or even a couple of days to get it right.

3. **Communicate.** Now that you are safely headed in the right direction and out of extremis, communicate with the team: "Here's the problem, and here's what we are going to do about it. These few things are your priority tasks right now." Contact others to ask for help if necessary. When it comes to alignment, effective communication is number one. Without constant, clear, and concise communication, the formation will disintegrate, and your goal will recede or disappear. (If you don't get the first two steps right, of course, all the talking in the world won't get you out of trouble—so keep your priorities straight!)

And remember: fighter pilots aren't born with the ability to prioritize tasks in a high-stress environment; *we learn the skills necessary to do so.* We learn to work through the strain and tension of task overload

Fighter pilots aren't born with the ability to prioritize tasks in a high-stress environment; *we learn the skills necessary to do so.*

—CAREY LOHRENZ

by using the simple, three-pronged message: Aviate, Navigate, Communicate. And we practice this relentlessly in preparation, in briefing, in simulators, in flight, and in our day jobs to greatly improve our execution—even in a crisis.

One Key Vision

Every aircraft carrier has about five thousand people on board, and every nine months there is a 50 percent turnover. That means every eighteen months you have an entirely new crew in what is known as the most dangerous industrial worksite in the world. Add the fact that the average age of those working on deck is nineteen years old, and well, you've got a potentially chaotic environment, to say the least.

That is why we had to be incredibly clear about our one key purpose for being there in the first place: support the successful launch and recovery of military airplanes twenty-four hours a day, seven days a week, three hundred and sixty-five days a year. Every individual understood that every action threaded to and tied back to that main purpose. This allowed everyone to understand that they each played a significant role in making that success a reality even amid fear of failure.

The best way to keep your team aligned is to boil down your vision into a *vision statement*: a tagline that reminds people of that full picture of success you're all working toward. When it's reinforced on a regular basis, that vision starts to get into everyone's subconscious. Without even thinking about it, you are pulled toward that vision; it determines your actions—the steps that you will take to get there.

For the Navy in its entirety, that vision is "We are an integrated Naval force that will provide maritime dominance for the Nation."

For the goose, I imagine, it's probably as simple as "We fly south together when the temperature drops."

What's yours?

In order to make the vision accessible at all times, your vision statement needs to be simple, memorable, and repeatable. This can be painstaking work; oftentimes the simpler the statement is, the more time somebody has spent crafting it. But if you want your vision to stick, it's really important to take the time to get it right. The more people you need to get behind you and the more complicated the steps ahead of you, the simpler and more memorable your vision statement needs to be. Make it succinct and transferable. It should communicate to people instantly, without explanation.

THE MORE PEOPLE YOU NEED TO GET BEHIND YOU AND THE MORE COMPLICATED THE STEPS AHEAD OF YOU, THE SIMPLER AND MORE MEMORABLE YOUR VISION STATEMENT NEEDS TO BE.

The vision statement should make the goal, mindset, and flight plan contagious.

Consider these fabulous examples:

- Southwest Airlines: "To become the world's most loved, most flown and most profitable airline."

- Ben & Jerry's: "Making the best ice cream in the nicest possible way."

- IKEA: "To create a better everyday life for the many people."

All clear-cut.

Complicated visions *do. not. work.* Keep the language focused and messaging clear. Then write it down. Put it where everyone can see it. Repeat it often.

CREATING A CONTAGIOUS VISION

Crafting a clear and concise vision statement is the best way to inspire all of those on your team and disseminate the purpose of the thing you are trying to accomplish.

Write down three key action words (common examples are *empower*, *engage*, *achieve*, *instill*, *develop*, etc.).

_____

_____

_____

Write down the three most important values (examples could be *health*, *maximum profit*, *product quality*, *environmentalism,* etc.).

_____

_____

_____

Who is your goal impacting? Is it just you? Your family? Your community? The world?

_____

_____

_____

_____

Why are you pursuing this goal? What is your purpose? Who are you here for?

_____

_____

_____

_____

What does the goal look like in five to ten years?

_____

_____

_____

_____

_____

Spend some time reviewing the above and circle the words you wrote down that resonate most with your goal. Now try writing your vision statement in the space given here. Try not to go beyond that limit.

_____

_____

_____

_____

_____

Clarify the Complex

In times of extreme chaos, speed really *is* life.

When it comes to:

- delivering predictable results,

- maintaining your and others' focus,

- seizing opportunities, and

- accomplishing your goals,

you must clarify the complex.

Reducing complex thoughts to clear and simple communications will not only keep you alive, it'll increase organizational and individual performance by aligning everyone's actions.

Whether it's communicating with your team, sharing a go-to market strategy with your sales force, or creating a mission-focused culture, being concise, precise, clear, and consistent is a game changer.

SAY WHAT YOU NEED TO IN AS FEW WORDS AS POSSIBLE SO THAT AS MANY PEOPLE AS POSSIBLE CAN UNDERSTAND.

In the Navy, we called this "comm brevity," which means you say what you need to in as few words as possible so that as many people as possible can understand.

Just like geese, pilots have their own unique form of communication. If you've ever boarded a flight and heard conversations going on in the cockpit, you probably didn't glean much from the exchange. But the phrases used by pilots and flight crew were borne out of a need for clear and succinct communication to all of those listening over an occasionally fuzzy radio transmission.

The aim is less wordy and more worthwhile communications.

Short and sweet. Clear and concise.

Terms like *angels* designate altitude in thousands of feet ("angels 6" is six thousand feet). When someone says, "Bingo," you might suspect it's not referring to a game, but do you also know it's not confirming a positive outcome or correct answer? In pilot speak, *bingo* indicates a low-fuel status, which might mean it's time to divert to a different airfield. And the radio call "Mooner, your signal is Buster Miramar" means *mooner* needs to head toward a particular airfield as fast as possible. No other communication required. There might be "pilot speak," but its value is that it communicates a specific meaning concisely, precisely, clearly, and consistently.

How can communicating complex ideas clearly help you in a difficult situation? Let's start with some simple recommendations for email communications:

1. Stop hitting "reply all" unless absolutely necessary.

2. BLUF. Bottom Line Up Front. Don't bury the most important piece of information three paragraphs into your *War and Peace*–style email.

3. Speak and write plainly. Please. Four-syllable words don't make you look or sound smarter than everyone else. And they certainly don't make whatever message you're trying to relay more relatable or actionable.

Nothing should need to be second-guessed or decoded. Comm brevity eases coordination and improves understanding. It helps provide a clear path to success, not one that can be misinterpreted or that opens up the channels for endless questioning at a time when taking correct action is the most important thing.

In the Navy, we had to figure out how to take a complex environment and net it down to the most important work.

The same is true for disseminating important and complex information during a crisis. Stress, uncertainty, and overwhelm demand a focused form of communication that is significantly different than communicating in routine, low-stress situations. Acting "business as usual" when everything is falling apart can lead to outcomes that are anything but aligned, accelerated, successful, and lifesaving.

When people are fearful or overwhelmed, the last thing anyone needs is to sift through muddled information and confusing jargon. It's not just that there's no time for making sense—it's that our capacity to make sense that is limited. Whether it's the daily press conferences during COVID-19, the responses to 9/11 or the 2017 Las Vegas shooting, *people in high-stress situations have difficulty digesting information*. And their recall and short-term memory are limited as well.

PEOPLE IN A STRESSED STATE OF MIND WILL LOSE, ON AVERAGE, 80 PERCENT OF THEIR CAPACITY TO PROCESS INFORMATION.

People in a stressed state of mind will lose, on average, 80 percent of their capacity to process information. Things like basic listening and being able to understand or remember what they see or hear goes out the door. Additionally, research has shown that less than five percent of public stress is driven by fact—meaning that 95 percent of public concerns are based on *perception*.[47] As you can imagine, this can lead to *major* misperceptions (and places way too much importance and validity on our uncle's friend's boss's daughter's social media posts).

Chaos and high-risk environments demand a particularly quick form of alignment and acceleration, as well as an understanding of what our default will be in those situations.

Dr. Vincent Covello, a behavioral neuro- and visual-scientist, and founder and director of the Center for Risk Communication, has spent years conducting comprehensive reviews on the best practices for communicating in high-risk environments.

Let's look at some of his points to remember about communicating in high-stress environments:

- There is a loss in ability to hear, understand, and remember information.

- People want to know that you care before they care about what you know. Caring is 50 percent of the basis for determining trust and is determined in the first thirty seconds. Once that assessment is made, people are highly resistant to changing their minds.

- People remember what they heard first and what they heard last.

- People typically understand information at four grade levels below their educational level.

- People actively look for visual or graphic information that supports verbal messages (the visual part of the brain becomes an active player in processing information).[48]

And now let's consider some of the best practices that come from these insights:

- Speak clearly and slowly.

- Anticipate, prepare, and practice.

- Establish trust by establishing that you care.

- Repeat the most important points.

- Balance each negative with three to four positives.

- The first and last things you say are most likely to be remembered.

- Speak in short sentences and use simple words.

- The optimum length of key messages is twenty-seven words in nine seconds, making three points.[49]

THE OPTIMUM LENGTH OF KEY MESSAGES IS TWENTY-SEVEN WORDS IN NINE SECONDS, MAKING THREE POINTS.

That last point is fascinating. Twenty-seven words. Nine seconds. *Three points*. The complex must be clarified and condensed.

Clarify (and condense) the complex.

You don't need an opening monologue. You don't need an inspiring introduction. You also don't need all the explanations right away. You need up-front facts that are focused on the matter at hand and that demonstrate a concern for general well-being.

Think of Franklin D. Roosevelt's advice: "Be sincere. Be brief. Be seated."

Clarity and brevity are the orange glowing meatball and center-line lights of a flight deck. They not only guide and align, but they allow you to focus on the thing at hand. **No matter how dark the circumstances, don't leave your communications to chance.**

CONDENSE YOUR MESSAGE

Twenty-seven words. Nine seconds. Three points. Consider a current message that needs clarifying. Try to limit your words and keep your message brief.

Point 1: _____

_____

_____

Nine-Word Description: _____

_____

Point 2: _____

_____

_____

Nine-Word Description: _____

_____

Point 3: _____

_____

_____

Nine-Word Description: _____

_____

Once you have your three points clarified to only nine words, summarize the points into a memorable "one, two, three" chain of information or action.

1. _____

2. _____

3. _____

Relentlessly Filter the Unnecessary

Steve Jobs knew how crucial a focused vision is in the professional world. Writing about his biography of the Apple leader in *Harvard Business Review,* Walter Isaacson said that many commentators sprang up around the book's release, hoping to derive management lessons from Jobs's life; some of these analyses were on target, others weren't. Among the real keys to Jobs's success, Isaacson points out, the very first was focus: "Focus was ingrained in Jobs's personality and had been honed by his Zen training," Isaacson writes. "He relentlessly filtered out what he considered distractions."[50]

One of the reasons Apple is such a great company is that it puts out beautiful, easy-to-use products. But if you think about it, another reason Apple is so successful is that everything the company makes can fit on one giant table. Ever visited an Apple store? If you took one of each of its products—iPad, iPod, iPhone, iMac, etc.—you would be able to carry the entire selection out of the store in one big shopping bag.

When Steve Jobs made his return to Apple in 1997, the company was nearly bankrupt—it had sixty days of cash left—and was producing dozens of different types of products and peripherals. Talk about a crisis. He shut down 1,040 projects and focused on four major categories: consumer, pro, desktop, and portable. Then he assembled his top one hundred teammates and brainstormed products, ideas, and what Apple should be doing next. They whittled the list down to a top ten, and then Jobs slashed that list further. He was famous (or infamous) for saying, "We can only do three!" Three products—that was it. It probably sounded crazy at first, but few can deny that Jobs's approach brought the company amazing success.

There it is again: *only three things.* That clarity and focus led to the Apple team's alignment.

If you're laser-focused on three things within your Span of Control, there's a pretty good chance that you are going to be successful at those three things, whatever they might be. That's especially true when you take care to focus your communication about those three primary things and set aside what's distracting or irrelevant.

Clarity of communication about our vision, our goals, and the steps toward achieving them involves eliminating what is *not* contributing to that effort as much as it requires succinctly delineating what is. That's even more true in a crisis: if there are things that aren't critical in getting you out of a crisis fast, throw 'em overboard.

Focus and clarity always win.

Trust me, if you are clear about where you are going together, you'll get there a whole lot faster.

FOCUS QUESTIONS

- Are you able to communicate your vision clearly and concisely? Right now try saying it out loud and recording yourself on your phone. Listen to the audio. Does it sound clear and inspiring? Would you want to align with that vision based on what you heard?

- Do you have people alongside you to accomplish your goals? If not, why?

- What is the one thing that you want everyone to walk away knowing about your vision?

Chapter 12

GO BEYOND POSSIBLE

There's a reason no one else in the world except US Navy and USMC fighter pilots will attempt to land high-speed fighters on and off of aircraft carriers at night—it's simply too dangerous. The high-risk, high-reward equation has been deemed unacceptable by most.

The problem is that risk is always there, no matter how much training or technology you invest in the situation. It's a troubling thought, isn't it?

It takes years of training before you make that first night carrier landing. And then we spend countless hours in lectures, simulators, flying, and briefing and debriefing, trying to derisk an exceptionally dangerous environment. As new pilots, "nuggets" in the fighter wing, we listen intently to war stories and "there I was" tales of terror, experience, and success, listening for the "gouge" (that's Navy slang for "insider info").

The list of things to avoid is a mile long: don't get low, that'll mean a ramp strike. Don't get high—if you chop (cut) the power to try to recover the approach, it can be a fatal mistake. Don't get on the back side of the power curve, your engines won't have enough time to spool up to maintain or gain altitude. Don't get low and slow. Don't "chase the deck" in a pitching deck situation no matter how much that meatball is moving. Don't trust what you feel or the things that you may see outside of your cockpit because the way your mind interprets them is patently false.

That's a lot of information and stress to manage when you're also working to stay disciplined enough to keep your cool. Throughout the constant decision-making and communications with our wingman and ship, there is rarely even a hint of emotion. Nothing but calm, collected confidence. If we all had heart-rate monitors strapped on, they would tell a different story.

We know things can go bad quickly when doubt, uncertainty, or panic creep in. As carrier-based naval aviators, we've all lost friends in their failed attempts to land. Even the best pilots can make a fatal mistake. And we've seen the footage as well—the visual is seared in our memories and can bubble back to the surface when the blanket of darkness settles in.

Nighttime flying is the worst. Everything feels more extreme, margins for mistakes almost nonexistent. You're double-checking, then triple-checking your settings, fuel states, engine readings, tanker positions. As you reach the point of dropping your landing gear and flaps, it's as though time either accelerates or comes to a standstill, as we are "in the zone."

Whatever you do, even if you're feeling desperate, you can't "spot the deck" because you'll land where you're looking. If you "spot the deck," that means you're looking (yes, even in the pitch dark, our instincts anxiously want to see and search for certainty) at the place you want to land, and you'll end up in the "spudlocker," i.e., below the actual flight deck landing area. It's a hideous event in which the pilot actually rams into the aircraft carrier somewhere between the water line and the top of the aft end of the ship.

It's worse than playing Russian roulette; the odds are not in your favor.

How does it happen? Spotting the deck occurs when you stop scanning your instruments and environment, and you fixate on that one spot where you want to land. Looking at the point of intended touchdown is a problem when you're already attempting to land in a very small area that is constantly moving away from you and at an angle. That's because the place you're trying to land simply will not be in that same spot a few seconds from now. You'll always land short of where you intend.

This makes sense if you think about it: our brains are working so hard to find one thing we can control or hold on to during times of uncertainty or crisis. But we have to keep our scans moving on the environment and the things we *actually* can control.

We do our best to stay mindful during times of stress. We work to properly compartmentalize, setting aside all unnecessary distractions. We expect adversity, but we also expect and resolve to thrive. This takes grit, the willingness to do the hard work, continually learning, and trusting that no matter what, you'll figure it out.

It's a mindset.

Fighter pilots were practicing mindfulness long before it was a thing.

FIGHTER PILOTS WERE PRACTICING MINDFULNESS LONG BEFORE IT WAS A THING.

Setting Your Sights

You know those vision tests at the eye doctor? The ones that have the big *E* on top and then eleven subsequent rows with an increasing number of letters that are smaller in size? It's called a Snellen chart

We do our best to stay mindful during times of stress. We expect adversity, but we also expect and resolve to thrive. This takes grit, the willingness to do the hard work, continually learning, and trusting that no matter what, you'll figure it out.

—CAREY LOHRENZ

(named after Dutch ophthalmologist Herman Snellen), and the goal is to measure your vision and focus.

The standard chart was originally placed at twenty feet away, which is why most of us have come to understand 20/20 as having *perfect* vision.

As you might imagine, there are strict vision requirements for flying multi-million-dollar machinery 40,000 feet in the air with varying levels of visibility or at Mach 2. Fighter pilots have to undergo rigorous testing to demonstrate their perfect 20/20 eyesight. That means you sit in that optometrist's chair and you read every little letter on that chart—no glasses, no contacts. That means no color-blindness and no fuzzy bottom line.

That requirement—and the commonly held belief that pilots have superior vision—was made the basis of a groundbreaking experiment conducted by Ellen Langer, PhD, renowned social psychologist and the first female professor to gain tenure in the Psychology Department at Harvard University.

Langer's research team tested the eyesight of a group of students from MIT's ROTC program—none were pilots at the time—then put them in the uniform and environment of a fighter pilot. They donned the students in green Nomex flight suits and placed them into a flight simulator, specifically instructing them to actively imagine themselves as pilots. The simulator consisted of an actual cockpit including all the bells and whistles mounted on hydraulic lifts that mimicked the aircraft movement and performance of a fighter jet.

The fact that the researchers would be testing their vision inside the cockpit was never mentioned to the new "pilots."

Langer simulated four aircraft approaching from the front, each with a serial number on the wing. The volunteers were told to read the serial numbers on the four wings, which, unbeknownst to them, were equivalent to the smaller lines on a Snellen chart.

Langer, secretly and smartly, was administering the optometrist's standard eye exam under the guise of her participants playing pilot.

A control group took the same initial vision test, then sat in the cockpit with the simulator turned off. They simply watched the computer-generated planes whir by and read the serial numbers as instructed.

What did she find? Unmistakably, the "pilots" showed improvement in their vision. Four out of the ten volunteers could see better when playing pilot. And how many of the "controls" who sat unmoving in their normal jeans and T-shirts demonstrated improvement?

Zero. Zilch. Nada.

But Langer and her team wanted to rule out any effects that motivation might have. They wanted to clarify the extent to which the vision improvement was a matter of mindset. So the researchers brought another group of people into the cockpit and asked them to read a brief essay on motivation. After people finished reading, they were given pep talks and told to "keep motivated" and "try hard to have better vision" to perform well in the vision test.

With the simulator inactive, they began their test. There was no improvement.

What does all of this mean? The study suggests that simply *believing* that pilots have good vision was enough to sharpen the volunteer pilots' eyesight.[51]

I guess *believing* really is *seeing*.

As you're probably thinking, that was an elaborate experiment. Plus the number of participants was small. Langer thought so too. So she decided to explore the question in a completely different way. In a second experiment, she tested the belief that athletes have good vision.

Langer tested the eyesight of a larger group of volunteers all with similar natural athleticism. She had some do jumping jacks while others simply skipped around the room. She wanted to balance the experiment by having all the participants be active but figured that psychologically, jumping jacks would be seen as more athletic than skipping.

When she retested their eyesight, a *third* of the jumping-jack volunteers had better vision, while only one of the skippers showed improvement. Remember, they all were physically similar. The only thing that differentiated the two groups was their psychological mindset as a result of jumping or skipping. That was enough to sharpen their view of the world.

Literally.

Langer didn't stop there, though. She ran a final experiment, this one taking advantage of the mindset primed by the traditional Snellen chart.

When we find ourselves getting our yearly checkup, many of us are used to getting more and more uncertain of our choices as the letters get smaller and smaller. We may expect to read the first few lines perfectly clearly, but by the third line, we can find ourselves at a total loss.

In her final experiment, Langer and her team showed people a "reversed" and "shifted" chart. At the top, it included letters equivalent in size to the letters on the third line, and the chart progressed to letters of very small size at the bottom. Because people were expecting to read the top few lines with ease, they were able to read much smaller letters as well. Overall, the volunteers saw letters that they normally couldn't see. Because they inherently believed they would be able to read the top of the chart, they did—regardless of the actual font size.[52]

What does all of this mean?

If mindsets really do affect and change us, maybe instead of being externally manipulated by subtle scientific priming, we can be more intentional with our thinking and do that reevaluation ourselves.

And instead of just positive reappraisal—seeing the good in things—we can try for *possible* reappraisal as a way of seeing what really is feasible for us when we take our limiting beliefs out of the picture.

Psychology can trump biology.

Belief can trump improbability.

Mindset can trump impossibility.

That goes for fighter pilots and "fighter pilots," athletes and "athletes," you and the *you* that you might become.

Leave Room for the Possible

Here's the lesson, y'all: you have more control than you think you do.

We've all done the limiting self-talk: "I'm just not good at math," "I could never play guitar like he does," "Girls don't do that kind of job," "Someone has already said it; I have nothing new to say," "I'm not strong enough," or "I'm not fast enough."

Sound familiar? These statements are all fear talking—and it's whispering self-defeating things. You take them to heart, even though you would never dream of saying such things to anyone else! Nine times out of ten, the fear is telling you a bullshit story—yet you believe it.

Our self-talk influences our mindset, abilities, talents, potential, and even intelligence.

So how do we boost our confidence to tilt toward what is possible? And how can we change the way we talk not only to ourselves but also our teammates, family, friends, and kids?

Assuming you've put in the time to prepare, perform, and prevail, a straightforward way to practice leaving room for the possible is to ask these questions:

- What is possible if you put in the work?

- What is possible if you're able to channel fear, frustration, passion, or anger?

- What is possible if you take action?

- What is possible if you try something new?

- What is possible if you succeed?

- What is possible to learn if you fail?

- What is possible if you channel your energy for a cause or purpose outside of your own?

- What is possible if you focus on your Span of Control?

The language you use to frame your experience will dictate your mindset around the possibility for success.

When struggling, tell yourself: "I just don't have it *yet*" or "We're not there *yet*." This sets up the possibility of success. Then continue to do the work, to take action, to learn, to improve, to get closer to discovering what is possible for you.

> THE LANGUAGE YOU USE TO FRAME YOUR EXPERIENCE WILL DICTATE YOUR MINDSET AROUND THE POSSIBILITY FOR SUCCESS.

Major Misconceptions

Here's a riddle I bet you'll never crack.

What do Napoleon Bonaparte, sleepwalkers, and dogs have in common?

Anybody?

Major misconceptions.

Anyone whose been accused of having "a Napoleon complex" probably wouldn't be considered the tallest guy in the room. When we think of Napoleon Bonaparte, the historical giant of France, we think of a short guy with a big ego, but it's based on very little fact. In truth, Napoleon was above average height in France at that time at 5'7".

And did you know that waking a sleepwalker won't hurt them? Sure, they may get a little disoriented (I mean, who wouldn't be if they went to sleep in their bed and woke up in the front yard), but it can't *physically* harm them.

And most of us think you multiply a dog's age by seven to calculate their comparable age in human years, but that's just a made-up number that's been circulating since the thirteenth century. There's nothing scientific (or true) about it.

The reality is that there are many things we believe to be true simply because we've heard them repeated and never thought to question whether they're fact or fiction. And we know now just how much beliefs play a huge part in how we see the world, move through it, and make decisions about our futures.

Typically, we think we form our beliefs by hearing something, thinking about it, and then converting our conclusion into a belief. However, psychologists tell us that when we hear something (true or not true), our brains are wired to intuitively believe it as a *fact*. That means disproving it later is incredibly difficult.

In 1993, Harvard psychologist Daniel Gilbert completed a series of experiments confirming that our default is to believe that what we hear and read is true. In the experiment, subjects were instructed to read a series of statements about a criminal defendant. These statements were color-coded to make it clear whether they were true or false. Subjects under time pressure or who had their cognitive load increased by a minor distraction made more errors in recalling whether the statements were true or false. But the errors weren't random. Under any sort of pressure, they believed *all* the statements were true, regardless of their labeling.[53]

First of all, this means that the more stressed out we are, the less likely we are to make informed and thoughtful decisions (so be careful making crucial decisions if you are too overwhelmed to think clearly). Second, and more important, Gilbert's research demonstrates how things we heard in the past and inherently believe to be true can, in turn, form our beliefs about what is possible for us.

Did Napoleon believe he was short?

Are sleepwalkers fearful of being woken up?

Are dogs missing out on important birthdays?

Think back on all the times you've heard that something isn't possible. Think back on all the times you haven't voiced an idea simply because you knew you would hear that it can't be done.

Every belief, including those you have about yourself, is learned and conditioned through experience. Maybe as a kid you were told that you had a problem paying attention, and you've believed it ever since. Not only have you believed it, but it has informed what you are and are not capable of. Eventually, it may even have become a defining feature of how you see yourself and understand the world around you.

Those decisions that you make and the actions that you take based on what you *believe* are your beliefs *embodied*. They create who you are. Think of it like this:

Belief + Action = You

In fact, the word *identity* was originally derived from the Latin words *essentitas*, which means *being*, and *identidem*, which means *repeatedly*. Your identity is literally your "repeated beingness."

If your actions are how you *embody* your identity, then when you make your bed each day, you embody the identity of an organized person. When you write each day, you embody the identity of a creative person. When you train each day, you embody the identity of an athletic person. Our actions are definitive because they are how we build habits—both good and bad.

By acting the part, the "pilots" and "athletes" in Langer's experiments defined what they were capable of. Playing their assigned roles made them feel *more* like what they were embodying. Of course, it was simulated—those volunteers weren't going to be flying any F-14 Tomcats that day or playing in a Superbowl—but it did have a psychological and physiological effect on moving them past their limitations.

I'll say it again because it's so important: your actions and habits matter. The more you repeat a behavior, the more you reinforce the identity associated with that behavior. The process of building habits is the process of becoming yourself.

EVERY CHOICE WE MAKE, WE ARE UNDERGOING A MICROEVOLUTION OF THE SELF.

Of course, evolution is gradual.

We do not change by snapping our fingers and deciding to be someone entirely new. Merely saying you are an athlete does not make you an athlete. Instead, we change bit by bit, day by day, activity by activity. Every choice we make, we are undergoing a microevolution of the self.

Every action you take is a vote for the type of person you wish to become. If you finish reading a book, then perhaps you are the type of person who likes reading. If you go to the gym, then perhaps you are the type of person who likes exercise.

Ultimately, you achieve what you believe. It comes down to learning from your failure and unlearning any tightly held beliefs that are holding you back. So many of us shortchange what we believe is possible for ourselves when, in fact, it's more likely we are capable of whatever it is we can think of.

So saying you are an athlete without putting in the work does not make you an athlete. But *believing* that you can be an athlete and then taking the proper *actions* to potentially become one (and sticking to them!) is what will make you an athlete.

That's why it's so important to direct your time and energy, your thoughts and your resources to solving the challenges that make the biggest difference for you.

FORMATIVE ACTIONS

Ask yourself: What actions have you taken today to get closer to the person you want to become?

First, write one word or phrase for what embodies the person you want to be. It could be author, CEO, talk-show host, or fighter pilot.

_____

_____

_____

_____

Then write down what you've done today and yesterday.

_____

_____

_____

_____

_____

_____

_____

Have any of the things you've done in the past two days contributed to you becoming that word you wrote down? If so, that's great! Keep going and see if you can add more tomorrow. If not, why? Write down exactly which things are keeping you from doing it.

_____

When we're confused about what we can and can't control, the pressures of life cascade down on us, and our sense of possibility shrinks. Our vision of the future fades into a pale shadow of what it truly could be. Our limiting beliefs become handcuffs.

OUR LIMITING BELIEFS BECOME HANDCUFFS.

But, friends, please listen: when you cut out all the distraction and focus on only the things you can control, right now, *your perception of your own potential grows*. Picture a garden full of nasty weeds. Only when you start to pluck out and dispose of the weeds that are literally choking the fruits of your labor will you begin to see that you can go beyond what you thought was possible.

I want to share with you one last rowing story that I think encapsulates all that we've covered. In 2019, the University of Washington Husky women's rowing team, seeded in fourth place heading into the NCAA Rowing Championships, showcased one of the most thrilling and ferocious comebacks in rowing history. The NCAA Championships are three grueling days of back-to-back world-class racing, netting the field down each day to only the fastest boats in the country.

By the final day of racing, all three Husky boats had earned a spot in the Division I Grand Final. At the halfway point in each Final race, each UW boat was trailing well behind. Remarkably, the varsity boat came from dead last (in sixth place) crossing through the 1,000-meter mark in the race and sprinted its way to the finish line, its bow ball crossing first.

All three finals were nail-biters. In each race, the Huskies ended up setting NCAA record times, with two of the eights winning by less than a second.

The team had now swept two NCAA titles in three years (they finished a close second the year before).

How did they manage this unprecedented feat of accomplishment? How do *you* find that extra gear when it may feel like success is slipping from your grasp?

One of my former college teammates happens to be their head coach. According to Head Coach Yasmin Farooq, a former University of Wisconsin–Madison coxswain, eight-year US National Team member, two-time US Olympian, Olympic team captain, and World Champion, it came down to their training, their mindset, their belief in each other, and a clear sense of what was possible. They stayed focused on their own boat and on what *they* could control.

When the team got to the starting line, they were racing for something bigger than themselves—they weren't simply "pulling together" but were pulling *for* one another. The heat prior to the final, the Texas boat had actually walked through them—so they knew Texas was fast, and they knew they were close. There was no margin for error.

They knew, too, that they could trust both themselves *and* each other. They had prepared and put in the work; they had studied and labored over their performance data, and they trained hard.

And then it was go-time. It was taking that excitement at the starting line and reframing butterflies to possibilities. It was about respecting the speed of the competition, and celebrating the opportunity to race. It was a wicked fast field—and it was the first time ever there were five teams that had qualified three boats in all three finals. It was exciting.

One of our sayings was, "We can only control ourselves, our boat, our lane."

Every boat rowed to an inspired performance. That last 500 meters was just sheer human will to win.[54]

They prepared. They performed. And by focusing on their Span of Control, they prevailed, going beyond what was expected of or predicted for them.

So often we are hedged in by boundaries, most of which are the mental barriers and limiting beliefs that we create. Then we justify poor results by claiming that they're due to limited time, limited money, limited talent, and limited options. Impossibility is a lie—all it takes to achieve your goals is a hell of a lotta effort.

MOOD FOLLOWS ACTION. EVERY. SINGLE. TIME.

Mood follows action. Every. Single. Time.

Remember, if some human has achieved your goal or something close to it, then you can too. Extend your own limits; go above and beyond the little box that you create for yourself. Even if your goal is something no one has done before, that does not mean it cannot be done. Goodness knows history is full of firsts when someone decided that something impossible could be done and did it. Not a humble brag, but *hellooo*, first female F-14 Tomcat fighter pilot of the US Navy here!

There will be obstacles, there will be barriers, and I promise you there will be setbacks. Sometimes you can put in the effort, you can perform at the top of your class, and there will still be things outside of your Span of Control that conspire to hold you back.

Stay tenacious. Stay gritty. Look for other ways to get done what needs to be done. Don't give up when there is still the possibility that you can be successful! If you stay engaged, if you continue learning, taking action, and believing in possibility—eventually you will find yourself in a position at the right time and under the right circumstances to be successful.

Take Control

If you look across every field, every industry, and every role—whether athletes or executives, fathers or mothers, students or entrepreneurs, fighter pilots or Army Rangers—the greatest leaders and the best performers will always be the ones who are willing to take risks. They are the ones willing to go beyond possible.

Why? They know what they want, they know what they can control, and they have a straightforward process to learn from mistakes and can therefore create more opportunities for themselves.

Taking risks will never be easy; it takes nerves of steel. If you have the courage to show up and go for it even when everyone else (and the negative-talking voice in your head) is telling you to pull back—if you can honor your voice and your instincts and your passions—you can write your own story.

Some of our boundaries are external influences like the market or the climate (both figurative and literal). These can dictate and shape the goals we have in place, but it's still up to us to figure out how we can work amid such serious constraints and limitations.

Here's the good news that I hope by now you're thinking along with me: you do not have to predict precisely what is going to happen in the future, and you can't control everything.

What you need to develop the capacity to do is step up and do everything you can to *build* a future for yourself.

This takes flexibility.

This takes resilience.

This takes discipline.

This takes work.

This takes clarity.

This takes practice.

This takes focus.

This takes others.

This takes *you* stepping up and engaging.

Don't wait for an invitation to make a difference in your life—it's not coming. And if you really, *really* need one, well, consider this it.

Think about what's *really* possible for you, and ask yourself to do just *one thing a day* that scares you a bit *and* puts you closer to your goal.

In order to solve this problem of chaos and make our goals, dreams, and commitments happen, we have to understand that to succeed when the pressure is on, we've got to know what we can and cannot control.

Span of Control is a tool, a framework, a compass, and a guiding force to help you harness possibilities, see opportunities, and take action. Span of Control helps you clarify the complex and navigate fear, ambiguity, and uncertainty one step at a time …

YOUR SPAN OF CONTROL FRAMEWORK

- Focus on what matters most. (Identify your top three things and remove distractions.)

- Formulate a flight plan for success. (Prepare, perform, prevail—never leaves success to chance.)

- Communicate what's possible. (Make it concise, precise, clear, and consistent.)

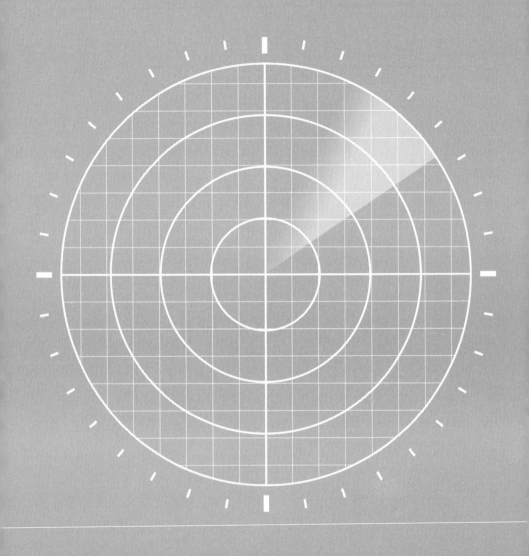

Conclusion

PUT THE LADDER DOWN

No one is self-made. No one.

Some people have had more challenging paths to success than others. But no one does it alone.

The single most important foundation for staying grounded during times of stress, uncertainty, and even crisis is to know history. Knowing history—the past beyond last week, last month, last year, or what any social media algorithm turns up—offers perspective on what can appear to be the overwhelming problems of the present.

History is what gives me confidence in my and your ability to weather any storm.

> **HISTORY IS WHAT GIVES ME CONFIDENCE IN MY AND YOUR ABILITY TO WEATHER ANY STORM.**

When you understand history—read the backstory, listen to the firsthand accounts and observations of struggles, and witness the endurance and achievements of those who have gone before you—everything should feel more ... doable.

Human history reflects our ability to be resilient, to innovate, to adapt and overcome. If we make the decision to read, study, listen, and learn, and then choose to step up and have a positive impact ourselves—overcoming adversity becomes more and more possible.

I'm often asked who inspired me, who my role models or mentors were, or what quotes I find inspirational. In order for me to give you my most honest answer to that question, I need you to join me in taking a step back in time.

I grew up just north of the spot where one of the world's biggest and best air shows is held, the Experimental Aircraft Association airshow in Oshkosh, Wisconsin. Every summer my dad would take my brother and me down to the show to meet some of his old squadron mates, climb over rare aircraft, and even chat with some real live pilots.

On only a handful of occasions did I ever meet female pilots. But on one sultry summer afternoon when I was about eleven years old, I met a WASP—one of the Women Airforce Service Pilots—a member of the amazing group of women who stepped into male military pilot roles during World War II. Little did I know at that time how her service, their service, would be the ladder that was put down for me.

In 1942, the United States was facing a critical shortage of pilots, the majority of whom were being sent to Europe or the Pacific for combat operations. After the bombing of Pearl Harbor, the rate of airplanes being produced had doubled, and more pilots were needed to test airplanes, train pilots, and ferry aircraft. Up to this point, women had never flown military aircraft. The decision was made to start a program first to see if women could serve as military pilots and, if so, then to train women to fly military aircraft so men could be released for combat.

The original program was called the Women's Auxiliary Ferrying Squadron, the WAFS, and was commanded by Nancy Harkness Love, a well-known commercial pilot and test pilot who had been working in a civil service position in the ferrying division at Air Transport Command in Washington, DC.

Initially, the standard for women even to apply to join the WAFS was astoundingly higher than for any men who wanted to fly for the military. Male applicants needed *zero* flight time logged to be considered for service. The women? They were required to demonstrate five hundred hours of prior experience. *Five. Hundred. Hours.* They also needed to hold a commercial pilot license with at least a two hundred horsepower rating (of note, two hundred horsepower airplanes had engines bigger than those in the military training command). That's not all: they were expected to personally kick in an additional $100 to cover uniform expenses.

General "HAP" Arnold, Commanding General of the US Army Air Forces, recognized that there was no way the US could ever find enough women with the entry qualifications that were demanded, so he authorized standing up a second squadron. This one was led by Jacqueline Cochran—an übertalented air racer and speed record–setter at the time—with application requirements that started at two hundred hours of flight time but were quickly reduced to thirty-five hours.[55] Even at thirty-five, the hours were used as a screen, an effort to eliminate applicants early, as if *not* having flight time was an indicator that the women lacked fitness or tenacity.

Eventually, the two separate women's squadrons merged and were renamed the Women's Air Force Service Pilots, the WASPs. The WASPs drew over twenty-five thousand applicants; 1,830 were accepted, 1,074 won their wings, and 38 lost their lives taking part in a wide range of domestic flying duties while serving their country. The WASPs ferried more than twelve thousand aircraft of seventy-eight types, flew more than two million hours, served *without military benefits*, and were paid less than half as much as the male civilian ferry pilots they had replaced.

Though not trained for combat, the WASPs flew a total of sixty million miles performing operational test flights, smoke laying, towing aerial targets with male gunners firing live ammo at them, transporting cargo, and a variety of other missions. By December 1944, the WASPs had flown every type of military aircraft manufactured for World War II and had a better safety record than the men who were doing the same jobs.

Propelled by passion and patriotism, the WASPs were willing to make the same sacrifices as their male counterparts for a lot less in return. They were all volunteers, civilians who—though their entry requirements were far greater—underwent the same rigorous physical training and testing that the men did. As you might imagine, they were frequently held to higher personal and professional standards than what were required of the men; they endured discrimination, false press reports, and outright sabotage.

THE WASPS PLAYED A CRITICAL PART NOT ONLY IN WINNING THE WAR BUT IN HANDILY DESTROY-ING THE NOTION THAT WOMEN COULDN'T FLY AS MILITARY PILOTS.

The WASPs played a critical part not only in winning the war but in handily destroying the notion that women couldn't fly as military pilots.

When the war was won and the men came home, the WASPs were told to pack up their gear, put away their leather jackets, and return home to be good wives, mothers, and sisters. Their presence and their service were no longer required.

To add insult to injury, the WASPs were not officially recognized as military pilots in the wartime effort.

This was an excruciatingly painful experience for the majority of women. For many, having the real value of their contribution dismissed and ignored devastated their core sense of self. They'd lost the very work that had provided them with teammates and friends, a sense of purpose, and a sense of their potential. Some never completely recovered from the feelings of heartbreak and having been betrayed.

They had dreamed big dreams, achieved esteemed flight status, and then had it all unceremoniously snatched away. Most WASPs looked for jobs in the aviation field, but even with hundreds (some thousands) of hours of experience, they were turned away. The industry hired only the men returning from war. The women were turned down repeatedly, not because they weren't qualified, but simply because of their gender.

Few shared their stories. Many dipped into despair.

There would be no place in history books for them, no GI Bill benefits to transform their lives, no plum aviation jobs, no healthcare benefits or services, no flags to put above mantels for those who lost a loved one in service. The United States seemed to forget that women ever flew. They were the forgotten heroines of World War II.

After the WASPs were disbanded, it would be another thirty years before women would once again be allowed to fly in military aviation, and those women would once again have to fight the same barriers, obstacles, and misperceptions as the women in World War II.

Decades passed until finally a handful of WASPs doubled down and lobbied Congress, the Senate, and the VA, year after year after year, to have their military service acknowledged.

Many spent the last years of their lives fighting for that recognition. In late 1977, President Carter signed HR 8701—the GI Bill Improvement Act—with an amendment "officially declaring the Women Airforce Service Pilots as having served on active duty in the Armed Forces of the United States for purposes of laws administered by the Veterans Administration." However, that bit of recognition was fraught with loopholes that still denied the WASPs most veterans' benefits.

So their fight continued.

It wasn't until June *2009* that Congress voted to give the WASPs the Congressional Gold Medal—the highest civilian honor Congress can bestow. The WASPs received the medal in a ceremony on March 2010 at the White House. By then, most of the women had already passed, never having been formally recognized or even acknowledged for their service and sacrifice.

The WASPs rose to the challenge of serving their country, and they did so while navigating uncharted waters, overcoming others' long-held beliefs that women couldn't fly, and overcoming barriers at every point during their service—airplanes being sabotaged, leadership that didn't support them, demands that they dare not go for the headline jobs, searing threats of violence if they dared to show up. They did so while being told to play small, to not appear too pushy, too demanding, too ambitious, too competent, too earnest in asking for what they earned.

Nevertheless, in spite, or because, of their collective experiences, they put the ladder down.

Just after they were recognized in the 1977 GI Bill Improvement Act, they stood up an association, the Women Military Aviators Association, to inspire, encourage, and empower current women military pilots while supporting those who had gone before. They reached out to offer words of encouragement, advice, and lessons learned to those who still found themselves one of few, if any, women in their squadron. Today the organization still exists—its mission is "to promote and preserve for historical, educational, and literary purposes the role of women pilots, navigators, and aircrew in the service of their country during times of war and peace."[56]

They turned their struggles into a shared strength, and they put the ladder down to help lift up the women who came after them.

I wish I would have known more fully of their stories, their experiences, and the challenges they overcame when I started flight school. All I knew then was that they had flown successfully. Without my understanding it fully, they were part of the reason I held an unshakable, deep belief from day one of training that "the jet doesn't know the difference." I figured as long as I performed well, nothing else mattered; any other discussions about gender and ability seemed like wasted energy to me. Women had flown in the military in the 1940s, for Pete's sake. *I knew I was standing on the shoulders of these women who had dared to go first.* It seemed insane to me that we were still having these "discussions."

I had a lot to learn. Still do.

Several years ago, after my military service, I was fortunate enough to serve on the board and then be president of the Women Military Aviators Association.

During that time, I also had the good fortune to deepen my friendships with some women who I had not only long admired but who had become great mentors as well. Their experience spanned not just years but decades—from aviators just a generation before me to the women who flew in the 1940s, the WASPs themselves. I wish I would have had those friendships, access to their stories, and that mentorship when I was still in the military. It would've made a lot more sense of what I was going through.

I remember a lengthy conversation with WASP Dawn Seymour at an aviation conference several years before she passed away in which she shared how after the WASP program shut down, she was so crushed that she packed all of her gear, her pictures, and her memories in a trunk and hid it away in a closet. For decades, she never shared her experiences—not with her friends, not her family, not even her kids. *No one* knew she had been a WASP. That trunk eventually moved to her bedroom, in the open, but no one was allowed to touch it, open it, or speak about it. Finally, in the 1970s, she went to her first reunion. But it wasn't until the 1980s that she felt strong enough to reestablish many of those relationships. Nearly forty years later, she finally shared with her kids the story of her service.

It's still the case that the overwhelming majority of Americans alive today have not even heard of the WASPs. Yet they and the women who followed them overcame, persisted, fought for recognition and for justice and for a fair shake, epitomized tact and unselfishness, defied judgment, took initiative against all odds, and, most important, were broken and responded to that by knitting themselves—and each other—back together.

How do you go beyond possible?

IT'S HISTORY THAT PROVIDES THE GREATEST REMINDER THAT WHEN YOU FOCUS ON YOUR SPAN OF CONTROL, ANYTHING IS POSSIBLE.

When you investigate and expand your sense of history, you learn to recognize and respect that *all of us* stand on the shoulders of those who have gone before, that there's a connection to the past when it comes to the purpose that drives us, the things we've endured, and what we can still accomplish. It's history that provides the greatest reminder that when you focus on your Span of Control, anything is possible.

For over thirty years, I've lived, studied, and researched leadership, high-performance behaviors, and risk management—in all kinds of organizations. I've seen the ways that true leaders lift others up and give them the supports they need to have a chance at success. At the end of the day, if we want to grow a country, an organization, a team, a family, a circle of friends, or ourselves and end up in a place more valuable and meaningful than where we are today? We need to put the ladder down.

We need to put the ladder down to bring people with us, to share our lessons learned, our strength, our capacity to endure.

We need to put the ladder down to pass on our expertise and our wisdom gained from both successes and tragedies.

When you leverage the power of Span of Control, apply it to your life and your decisions, and then share those skills and lessons with those around you? Anything is possible.

Understanding how we respond to stress and uncertainty and then being intentional about choosing a positive response—that's what allows us to navigate the present moment, to guide ourselves and our teams through challenging times, and to set up for success those who come after us.

When you leverage the power of Span of Control, apply it to your life and your decisions, and then share those skills and lessons with those around you? Anything is possible.

—CAREY LOHRENZ

ACKNOWLEDGMENTS

This book is the culmination of years of research, conversations in hallways, in interviews, in strategy sessions, on coaching calls with clients, backstage, and with teams around the world. I'm grateful to those who were brave enough to share their stories, their fears, their wisdom, and their insight.

Thank you to the clients and audiences along the way who have listened, internalized, shared, and harnessed their lessons learned and then rocketed into what is possible.

Anything noble and worthy that I've learned or done has come from the investment of others in me, in their belief in my potential when I didn't see it, combined with my own belief that if you're willing to learn, if you're willing to be coachable, and to fall and get back up—anything is figureoutable.

To Clint Greenleaf and the team at Content Capital, thank you. Clint, thank you for encouraging me to write this book, for your no-BS advice, and for forcing me to always level up. Thank you for getting this idea, and me.

To the team at Zilker Media, thank you for being a grand partner.

To my editorial team including Lauren Hall, Jen Holt, and Laura

Rashley, you made every page better, thank you. Thank you to the team at ForbesBooks, well done.

Thanks to Laura Gassner-Otting and Clay Hebert for picking up the red pen, reviewing a draft, asking the tough questions, and bringing the fun.

To my hard-working team at SpeakersOffice. Led by the divine Holli Catchpole—Jennifer Canzoneri, Tracey Bloom, Cassie Glasgow, Kim Stark, Michele Wallace, and Jessica Case, thank you. You all are magical, generous, and dedicated to making an impact on millions of people—faces you may not see, voices you may not hear, paths you may not cross—but they are there. And you are the guide. I am grateful to be on Team SO.

To my speaker bureau partners and friends, thank you for your years of friendship, business, for believing in me and my work, and for always being great wingmen.

Thank you to my loyal friends who continue to challenge me to show up; your friendship is a constant source of inspiration.

And of course, profound thanks to my family. Thank you for always believing in me, for using my own advice against me when I ran into roadblocks (strong move), and for being a constant reminder of what is possible with a world-class hype squad by your side. It's a gift I'll forever be working to repay. I love you.

And to you, dear reader, listeners, clients, and friends. I hope this book will serve you well over the years. Life can be brutal, but there is wisdom—and joy—to be found in our shared stories, shared lessons learned, and shared friendships.

I am beyond grateful for the generosity of your time, and the gift of your attention. Now it's up to you to have the courage—and vulnerability—to focus on your own span of control, and put the ladder down for the next person.

ENDNOTES

1   "Men and Heart Disease," Centers for Disease Control and Prevention, accessed January 15, 2021, https://www.cdc.gov/heartdisease/men.htm.

2   "The Illusion of Multitasking Boosts Performance," Association for Psychological Science, November 13, 2018, https://www.psychologicalscience.org/news/releases/the-illusion-of-multitasking-boosts-performance.html.

3   Gloria Mark et al., "No Task Left Behind? Examining the Nature of Fragmented Work," CHI 2005, April 2005, https://www.ics.uci.edu/~gmark/CHI2005.pdf.

4   Gloria Mark et al., "Email Duration, Batching and Self-Interruption: Patterns of Email Use on Productivity and Stress," CHI 2016, May 2016, https://affect.media.mit.edu/pdfs/16.Mark-CHI_Email.pdf.

5   Kermit Pattison, "Worker, Interrupted: The Cost of Task Switching," Fast Company, July 28, 2008, https://www.fastcompany.com/944128/worker-interrupted-cost-task-switching.

6   Larry Kim, "Multitasking is Killing Your Brain," Mission.org, January 26, 2016, https://medium.com/the-mission/multitasking-is-killing-your-brain-79104e62e930#:~:text=MIT%20neuroscientist%20Earl%20Miller%20notes,switching%20encourages%20bad%20brain%20habits.

7   Julien Laloyaux et al., "Research: Women and Men Are Equally Bad at Multitasking," *Harvard Business Review*, September 26, 2018, https://hbr.org/2018/09/research-women-and-men-are-equally-bad-at-multitasking.

8   Sofie Bates, "A decade of data reveals that heavy multitaskers have reduced memory, Stanford psychologist says," *Stanford News*, October 25, 2018, https://news.stanford.edu/2018/10/25/decade-data-reveals-heavy-multitaskers-reduced-memory-psychologist-says/.

9   "2017 NBAA Top Safety Focus Areas," NBAA, accessed January 15, 2021, https://nbaa.org/aircraft-operations/safety/2017-nbaa-top-safety-focus-areas/.

10   Walter Kintsch and John T. Cacioppo, "Introduction to the 100th Anniversary Issue of the Psychological Review," *Psychological Review* (101), no. 2, https://web.archive.org/web/20160303215911/http://psychology.uchicago.edu/people/faculty/cacioppo/jtcreprints/kc94.pdf.

11   Todd Spangler, "Video Streaming to TVs Soared 85% in US in First Three Weeks of March, Nielsen Says," *Variety*, March 31, 2020, https://variety.com/2020/digital/news/video-streaming-tvs-us-data-coronavirus-nielsen-1203550256/.

12   "US online alcohol sales jump 243% during coronavirus pandemic," Market Watch, April 2, 2020, https://www.marketwatch.com/story/us-alcohol-sales-spike-during-coronavirus-outbreak-2020-04-01.

13   Leslie Patton, "Americans Are Flocking to the Safety of Comfort Foods," Bloomberg, March 19, 2020, https://www.bloomberg.com/news/articles/2020-03-19/with-virus-lurking-americans-flock-to-safety-of-comfort-foods.

14   Amy Morin, "7 Scientifically Proven Benefits of Gratitude," Psychology Today, April 3, 2015, https://www.psychologytoday.com/us/blog/what-mentally-strong-people-dont-do/201504/7-scientifically-proven-benefits-gratitude.

15   Rick Hanson, *Hardwiring Happiness: The New Brain Science of Content-ment, Calm, and Confidence* (Harmony, 2013).

16   "Light-Emitting E-Readers Before Bedtime Can Adversely Impact Sleep," Brigham and Women's Hospital, December 22, 2014, press release, https://www.brighamandwomens.org/about-bwh/newsroom/press-releases-detail?id=1962.

17   Nancy Colier, *The Power of Off: The Mindful Way to Stay Sane in a Virtual World* (Sounds True, 2016).

18   John Rampton, "4 Proven Ways to Deal with Stress without Shutting Down, Giving Up or Taking Meds," Entrepreneur, August 25, 2017, https://www.entrepreneur.com/article/299225.

19   "Stress and Sleep – How to Master Stress and Enjoy Restful Sleep Instantly," The American Institute of Stress, June 12, 2018, https://www.stress.org/stress-and-sleep-how-to-master-stress-and-enjoy-restful-sleep-instantly.

20   Sleep Foundation, accessed January 15, 2021, https://www.sleepfoun-dation.org/.

21   Benjamin E. Hilbig, "Sad, thus true: Negativity bias in judgments of truth," *Journal of Experimental Social Psychology* 45(4), July 2009, https://www.sciencedirect.com/science/article/abs/pii/S0022103109000936?via%3Dihub.

22   Allison Ledgerwood, "A Simple trick to improve positive thinking," TEDxUCDavis, May 2013.

23   Kateri McRae et. al., "Increasing positive emotion in negative contexts: Emotional consequences, neural correlates, and implications for resilience," Positive Neuroscience, 2016.

24   Eric Garland et. al., "The Role of Mindfulness in Positive Reappraisal," *EXPLORE* 5(1), January 2009, https://www.ncbi.nlm.nih.gov/pmc/articles/PMC2719560/.

25   Emily Nagoski and Amelia Nagoski, *Burnout: The Secret to Unlocking the Stress Cycle* (Ballantine, 2019).

26   Jim Collins, *Good to Great: Why Some Companies Make the Leap ... and Others Don't* (HarperBusiness, 2001).

27   Carol Dweck, *Mindset: The New Psychology of Success* (New York: Random House, 2006).

28   Courtney E. Ackerman, MSc., "What is Resilience and Why Is It So Important to Bounce Back?" Positive Psychology, January 9, 2020, https://positivepsychology.com/what-is-resilience/.

29   R.G. Tedeschi and L.G. Calhoun, "Posttraumatic Growth: Conceptual Foundations and Empirical Evidence," *Psychology Inquiry* 15(1), https://psycnet.apa.org/record/2004-11807-003.

30   James B. Stockdale, Stockdale on Stoicism II: Master of My Fate, https://www.usna.edu/Ethics/_files/documents/Stoicism2.pdf.

31   "Job IQ Test," Wonderlic, accessed January 15, 2021, https://sample-wonderlictest.com/quiz/full-quiz/question/2.

32   Ryan Holiday, *The Obstacle Is the Way* (Portfolio, 2014).

33   Jeff Wise, "What's the Scariest Part of a Frightening Experience?" Psychology Today, March 11, 2010, http://www.psychologytoday.com/blog/extreme-fear/201003/whats-the-scariest-part-frightening-experience.

34   "span of control," definition, Lexico, accessed January 15, 2021, https://www.lexico.com/definition/span_of_control.

35   Matthew Pinsent, *A Lifetime in A Race* (Ebury Publishing), Kindle edition, p. 116.

36   Timothy J. Buschman and Earl K. Miller, "Top-Down Versus Bottom-Up Control of Attention in the Prefontal and Posterior Parietal Cortices," *Science* 315(5820), March 30, 2007, https://science.sciencemag.org/content/315/5820/1860.

37   John Szramiak, "This story about Warren Buffett and his long-time pilot is an important lesson about what separates extraordinarily successful people from everyone else," Business Insider, December 4, 2017, https://www.businessinsider.com/warren-buffetts-not-to-do-list-2016-10.

38   "Are SMART Goals Dumb?" Leadership IQ, accessed January 15, 2021, https://www.leadershipiq.com/blogs/leadershipiq/35353793-are-smart-goals-dumb.

39   Selina Hastings, "The Courageous, Intransigent Antoine De Saint-Exupery," *The New Yorker*, November 29, 1994, https://www.newyorker.com/magazine/1994/12/05/lost-in-the-stars.

40   Shainna Ali, PhD, LMHC, "Why New Year's Resolutions Fail," Psychology Today, December 5, 2018, https://www.psychologytoday.com/us/blog/modern-mentality/201812/why-new-years-resolutions-fail.

41   Mark Murphy, "Neuroscience Explains Why You Need to Write Down Your Goals If You Actually Want to Achieve Them," *Forbes*, April 15, 2018, https://www.forbes.com/sites/markmurphy/2018/04/15/neuroscience-explains-why-you-need-to-write-down-your-goals-if-you-actually-want-to-achieve-them/?sh=6ed402c37905.

42   Gert-Jan Pepping, Geir Jordat, and Tjerk Moll, "Emotional Contegion in Soccer Penalty Shortcuts: Celebration of Individual Success Is Associated with Ultimate Team Success," *Journal of Sports Sciences* 28(9): 983–92.

43 Scott Shappell et. al., "Human Error and Commercial Aviation Accidents: A Comprehensive, Fine-Grained Analysis Using HFACS," Report Number DOT/FAA/AM-05/24 (Washington, DC: Office of Aerospace Medicine, 2006), https://www.faa.gov/data_research/research/med_humanfacs/oamtechreports/2000s/media/200618.pdf.

44 Raymond B. Huey, "Mountaineers on Mount Everest: Effects of age, sex, experience, and crowding on rates of success and death," *PLOS ONE*, August 26, 2020, https://journals.plos.org/plosone/article?id=10.1371/journal.pone.0236919.

45 Harry Clarke Noyes, "The Goose Story," *ARCS NEWS 7* (1), January 1992.

46 Lara Sorokanich, "Still looking for Clorox wipes? Here's how the company has innovated to meet unprecedented demand," Fast Company, November 10, 2020, https://www.fastcompany.com/90572398/still-looking-for-clorox-wipes-heres-how-the-company-has-innovated-to-meet-unprecedented-demand.

47 "Crisis and Risk Communication Solutions," Center for Risk Communication, accessed January 15, 2021, http://centerforriskcommunication.org/environmental-risk-communications.

48 Vincent T. Covello and Patricia A. Milligan, CHP, "Risk Communication-Principles, Tools, & Techniques," United States Nuclear Regulatory Commission, accessed January 15, 2021, https://www.nrc.gov/docs/ML1015/ML101590283.pdf.

49 Ken Makovsky, "Communications in High Stress Environments," *Forbes*, October 3, 2013, https://www.forbes.com/sites/kenmakovsky/2013/10/03/1159/#bca4fae72700.

50 Walter Isaacson, "The Real Leadership Lessons of Steve Jobs, *Harvard Business Review*, April 2012, https://hbr.org/2012/04/the-real-leadership-lessons-of-steve-jobs.

51 "Do you really need those eyeglasses?" Association for Psychological Science, April 2, 2010, https://www.psychologicalscience.org/news/ were-only-human/do-you-really-need-those-eyeglasses.html.

52 Ozgun Atasoy, "Your Thoughts Can Release Abilities Beyond Normal Limits," Scientific American, August 13, 2013, https://www.scientificamerican.com/article/your-thoughts-can-release-abilities-beyond-normal-limits/.

53 Daniel Gilbert et. al., "You Can't Not Believe Everything You Read," *Journal of Personality and Social Psychology* 65(2), August 1993, danielgilbert.com/Gilbert%20et%20al%20(EVERYTHING%20YOU%20READ).pdf.

54 Yasmin Farooq, conversation with author, December 30, 2020.

55 "Report on Women Pilot Program," WASP on the Web, accessed January 15, 2021, http://www.wingsacrossamerica.us/wasp/final_report.htm.

56 Women Military Aviators, Inc., accessed January 15, 2021, www.womenmilitaryaviators.com.